1

Like
HELL!

*I live with pain--
and have a good
life, anyway!*

Ellen Lenox Smith

 **WOW! Books**

IT HURTS LIKE HELL
© 2016
By ELLEN LENOX SMITH

For information visit www.WOW-Books.com

Book Cover design by : Nitsan Gaibel
Interior Design by : Melissa@TheWriterLab.com

WOW Books Publishing

ISBN 13 : 978-0692677278
ISBN 10 : 0692677275

First Edition: MONTH 2016

Dedication

This book is dedicated to those that have encouraged me to keep fighting on with my life:

My husband Stu, sons Timothy, Ryan, Benjamin and Christopher, their wives Shaina, Cathleen, Alison and Amy, service dog Maggie, my physical therapist through the years - Kevin Muldowney, Linda Letourneau, Mike Healy and Patricia Meegan, along with family and friends that have kept caring.

Contents

Taste My World

My Good Life

In time, I learned that **not** focusing on me and my difficult journey was the trick to get my emotions away from my losses. Through the help of good friends that have not given up on me and my family to support me, we have found inner strength to cope better with our situation.

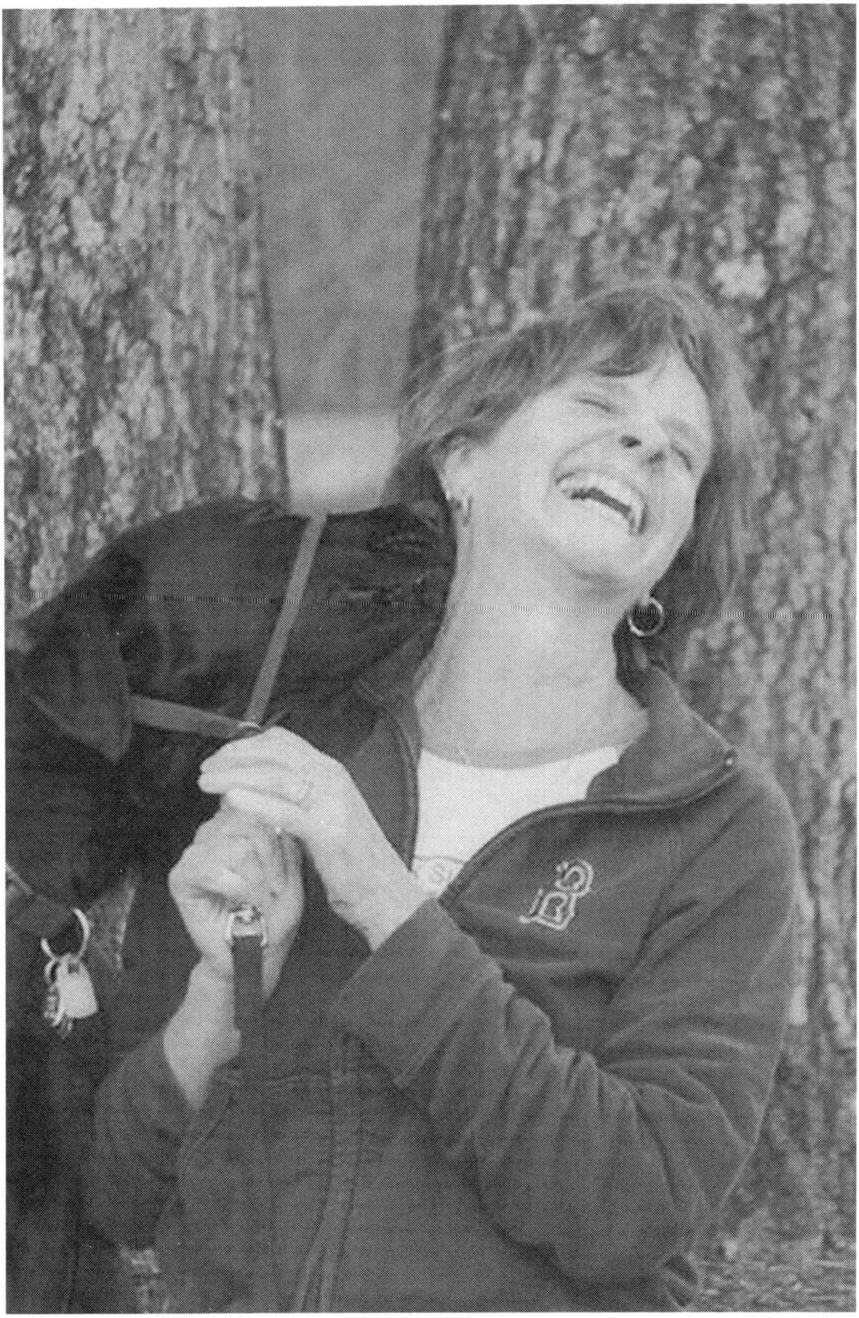

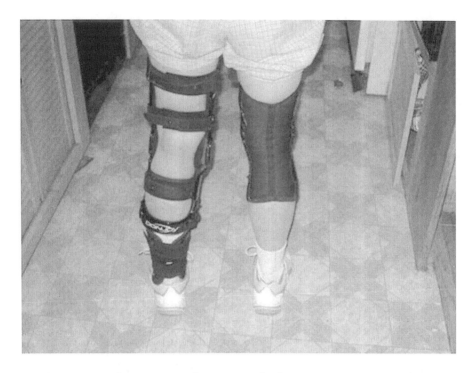

Pain—What I Live With Every Day ... And What Joys I Have To Give Up Forever

There is nothing more heartbreaking than to slowly experience your life deteriorate. I have now have had twenty-three surgeries to endure. I can no longer drive, walk on an uneven ground or the beach or my feet and legs sublux. I have lost my dream job of being a teacher, a high school swim coach along with being a master swimmer. And imagine not being able to lift more than five pounds so holding my own treasured grandchildren is not possible. And every night I go to bed, I hope that the trachea will not cut off that breathing to the point of taking my life away too soon.

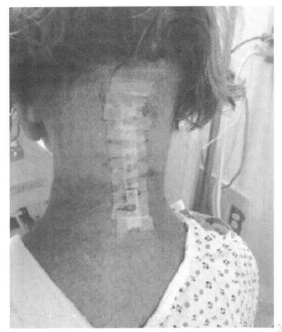

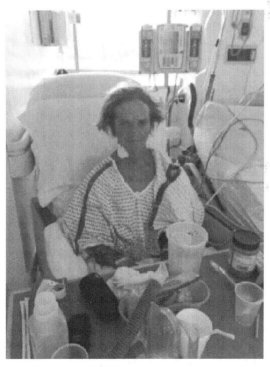

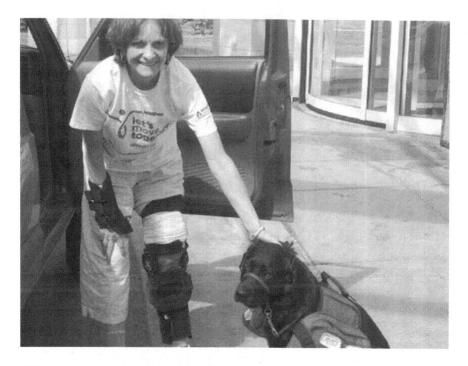

How Others' Help Has Made All The Difference

With the help from family and friends, I have learned that life can improve and regain value, that I thought I had lost. I had to learn to accept help and then quickly realized it helps to add humor to our lives, to help us all be comfortable with our new way of life. My husband, Stu, has been my rock and I wonder if I ever could have been this person without his love and support. My children, now all adults, have kept us laughing, feeling loved and supported. And Maggie, my service dog, is alongside me in every step of the life I now live, alerting me when I stop breathing among many other services she provides.

Giving To Others Relieves The Pain And Gives Meaning To My Life

Explaining to children how a service dog changes a life and is always helping their master, performing critical tasks for that person. "Next time you see one, don't run up to it and disturb it. It is on duty."

My husband and I spend many days advocating for various issues along with supporting others living with pain.

We are Arthritis Ambassadors, US Pain Ambassadors, as co-directors of medical marijuana advocacy, along with being on the board and both are on the board for RIPAC, RI Advocacy Coalition. We testify at home and travel to DC,meet with our congressman to advocate for causes and have had the honor twice to speak at FDA.

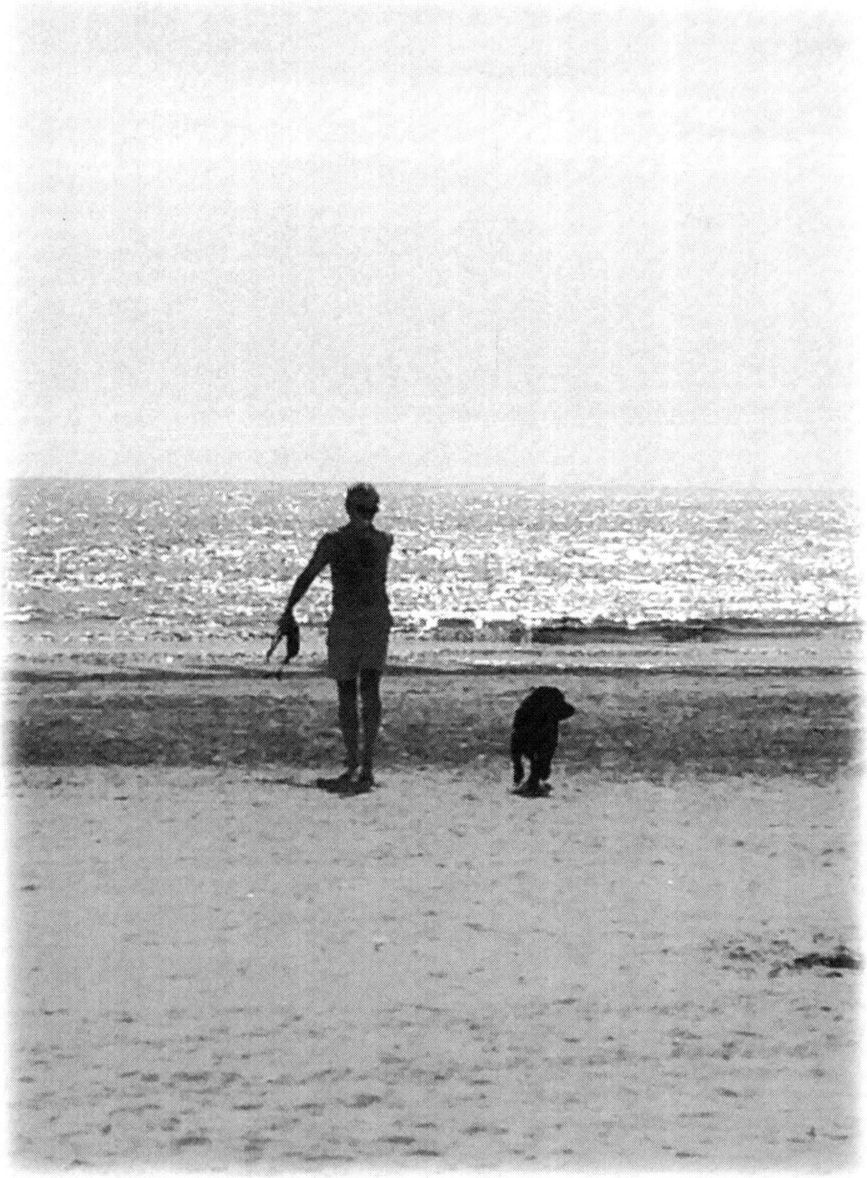

54

Imagine waiting for fifty-four years to understand what is going wrong with your body, only to find out that it is incurable and considered extremely rare. I had truly dreamed that with time, I would put the pieces of my puzzle together and get me fixed – never did it occur to me that I was about to face a life with what are presently considered incurable conditions. I have Ehlers-Danlos Syndrome, a lonely, misunderstood and doubted diagnosis where you are pretty much expected to find your own network of help. Support, compassion and guidance are rare to find in the medical world due to lack of understanding. Therefore, I sadly found myself wishing I had been diagnosed with something like cancer, so I could receive the compassion, a treatment plan, understanding and support from others instead of the judgment I have even felt from even some of my own family. After years of searching for a cure and diagnoses for my symptoms, I instead discovered that I was doomed to a life with not only pain but also doubting by others due to this being so rare and yet looking so normal. As if this wasn't enough, within two years, I was also diagnosed with sarcoidosis, another condition that has a chance of spreading and with no cure. So, how was I to make something of this new life I was destined to live?

This news is just not something you can ever emotionally prepare for – the news seemed inaccurate, impossible and wrong. But, after visiting three geneticists to confirm Ehlers-Danlos, it was clear that this was me – loose joints, subluxations, tearing with no warning, constant pain, foggy brain, and decisions for surgery after surgery to try to hold the joints together. Despite living a good life as a happy person that included daily exercising as a master swimmer and walking distance, eating from our organic garden, loving my career as a middle school teacher, and high school swim coaching, life was clearly going to be extremely challenging for the future. This story of my journey will share the trials and tribulations of learning HOW to live my life with humility, dignity, and better quality, despite these diagnoses. Giving up and being miserable was not going to be my solution!

Incurable Diagnosis

Trust me, you never have it in your bag of tricks on how to cope with being told you have incurable conditions. You spend each day trying to live life and then someone tells you it will most likely be cut short and will be a pretty painful journey to ride out. How are you supposed to begin to prepare to live this new life?

I quickly learned to live by four rules:

1. We all get something to cope with and this just happens to be the "gift" I was given.

2. I would waste my time if I got stuck on "why me". People really don't want to be around whiners, so that act had to be cleaned up quickly or I stood the chance of losing the friends I cared about.

3. I never stop being a parent, so although my four sons are now grown and out of the house, they were still observing how I am handling this and each of them has a 50% of also having EDS – so I need to be strong and continue to try to be a positive parent model.

4. This is it – the only life I get to live so I can choose to be miserable or move forward despite this. Happiness is an attitude – we either make ourselves miserable or happy and strong. The amount of work is the same! I choose life!

My husband and I have learned to listen to others and not judge the book by the cover. My condition of Ehlers-Danlos is considered an invisible condition; so we look normal to others until we have our braces on to hold our joints together or ride in our wheelchair when the legs are not cooperating.

After adopting that philosophy, I then realized that my teaching career was done. I no longer had the endurance to cope, despite adoring my career. In order to get emotionally prepared to retire, I began writing poetry. I found this process so cleansing yet also odd for I was not one that really enjoyed even reading much poetry. But, it seems that a muse visited me and after writing over ninety poems, I was ready to hear myself say the word "retirement" out loud and in doing so, realized that I was at peace with the only decision that made sense. With that decision in the process, the next thing I needed to help myself with was to get educated about my condition. I quickly found out the National Institute of Health was conducting research on EDS and was looking for subjects. I bugged them monthly for a year until I was contacted that I was accepted in. As others went off the spring of 2006, for their school break, I excitedly went off to Baltimore, for a five-day visit in a hospital to become part of the NIH research. I learned a lot during those days, much which was terribly disconcerting, but information needed to know to learn how to more safely live the life I was expected to now live.

My first attempt on expressing my emotions through words:

I Attended A Concert This Morning   10/17/06

It was that time to escape, to go for an adventure. We were attending a concert. All ten of our legs got into the car to begin the trip. No clues had been provided to us to prepare us for what an impact this performance would have on the rest of our day

We arrived, opened the door and got out, some of us more easily than others, and then shut the door off from life as we knew it...............

It seems that we were late for the concert. It was already in progression. We knew when we arrived that we would have to follow the rules. We had to turn off everything from our lives; the cell, the TV, the radio, computer and most importantly, "the mind".

We began to walk and quickly heard the concert. It felt loud and overwhelming at first. It felt crowded listening to it despite a lot of space provided, it was too much to hear, too much to absorb. And "the mind", it wanted to come on, even though it knew it wasn't invited. But it seemed to finally learn how to respect the rule. As it cooperated, the concert began to take on a new dimension of sounds and feelings. It became soft, clearer, calmer and incredibly comforting. This concert became exceptional, being absorbed in every space of the mind and body.

And all that was needed to feel this was to just turn off everything else.

The concert never came to a close, but it was time we return to the car and journey back to home as we know and love it. But, we knew we had had an experience that gave us strength and renewal to our lives. My dogs Corey and Carmel and Mom all took a moment to enjoy nature and listen to the truth of life. It was a concert that will never be forgotten. A

15

lesson was learned, "turn it all off", attend the concert of nature. It's there for us all and is open at all times.

As time moved forward and confidence crept into me with the help of my poetry, it was time to meet with my school principal and announce my retirement. She was truly shocked with my news, fully expecting that I was requesting the meeting to set a return date from my latest surgery. To my surprise, I was given a surprise party a few weeks later, at the end of a class I was attending in my school building. I, to this day, can't get over the fact that I was able to address the staff and hear myself securely say, "I am at peace with this decision." And the truth is, I was..........that chapter of my life was to be put aside, cherished in wonderful memories, but teaching in this capacity was no longer something I would have the endurance for again!

So, the trauma of resigning from teaching that I loved and sometimes, how I would define myself, was to be no more. It was a strange feeling to adjust to and I knew I would not be satisfied with life if I didn't quickly find something else to fill this huge gap I was to now face. So, in my research, I learned that EDS is actually under the Arthritis umbrella, as the rarest of one hundred types. My husband and I quickly contacted the foundation and offered our volunteer services. In a short time, in 2007, we had ourselves signed up as Rhode Island Arthritis Ambassadors. The assignments were fun, clear and ones that actually got me out of the house with my husband, Stu, to town hall meetings, dinners, state house testifying, calls to the DC offices of our representatives and in time, trips yearly to DC for the Arthritis Summit. It was wonderful to go from the responsibility of approximately 125 students daily to having something else worthwhile to focus on. However, in time, I realized this just wasn't enough for me. So within the end of my first year of retirement, we ended up also joining the American Pain Foundation in 2008, also as RI Ambassadors. This responsibility also required assignments to be accomplished and along with that, yearly paid trips for their summit. (Unfortunately, that foundation shut down this past summer of 2012.)

The US Pain Foundation was renamed from the CT Pain Foundation due to the founder, Paul Gileno creation of the Invisible Project. This is a traveling project that features various types of painful conditions through the subjects' photos and their story told. I read about this on facebook and quickly contacted Paul to offer myself for the condition of Ehlers Danlos. This just opened up many doors. Paul Gileno, founder and president of the

17

foundation and Nicole Hemmenway, the other co-founder and author of "No, It Is NOT In My Head," became our friends as we began a journey with them on working together to help others in pain. Stu and I also became a US Pain Foundation Ambassador and in time were even invited to speak about living in pain and he as my caregiver. By 2013, along with being a board member, our titles were changed to Co-Directors of Medical Marijuana Advocacy for the foundation.

Borrowed Time   11/15/06

We all use borrowed time
Each day we awake
Each step we take
Each sound we hear
Each taste
Each laugh
Each touch
It's all on borrowed time

We need to remember that each of these is a gift
We need to treasure what we have been given
We need to find the good in our moments traveling through life
For, these are borrowed times we've been given

Some of us will have a lot of time to borrow
Some of us will have ours cut short
But what we have in common is the gift of the time we have been given
Remember, it's borrowed time
Make the best of your gift

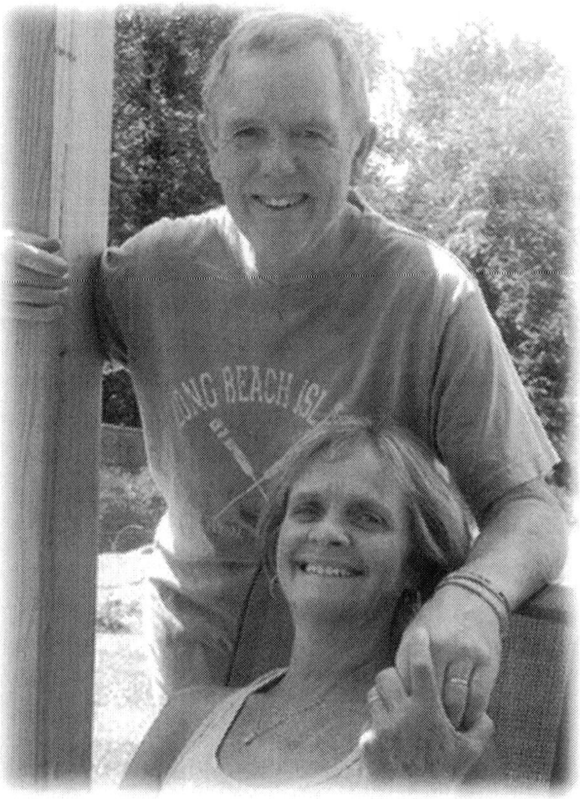
ONG BEACH ISL

Develop Your Network
Of Support

One of the first things you need to establish is a network of medical people. Coping with any rarer condition can make this task extremely difficult to achieve. I have been to many that are considered the best in the area and have walked out of the appointment knowing I will never return. The message is clear to me when someone sits there and tells me "I look fine and am breathing just fine". Clearly that statement tells me they are not vested at all in trying to help me. Many conditions are considered invisible, so others will not understand what you are really dealing with. But to have a medical staff make that comment alerts me that I need to keep searching. I can't tell you how many appointments I have gone to with an open mind and excitement that this may be the person that will get on board and try to help me. And, I can't tell you how many times I have returned home discouraged that this was just another dead end.

What I have done with Ehlers-Danlos patients that are referred to me by physicians is to invite them over, discuss the condition, answer any questions I can to help guide them and send them home with a list of doctors that I have found that are willing to listen, think out of the box and get on board to try to help EDS. I know there is only so much that can be done with this bizarre condition, but just to have someone listen, compassionate and try means the world to me. We don't need more people making us feel that we are nuts, making this up and attempting to just seek attention. That is such an insulting feeling to deal with when you already don't feel well and are just trying to cope living life. So, get a good support group that you can turn to when needed!

Vessel 2/14/07

A vessel,
A utensil for holding something
It is not responsible for what is inside
It is just the protector, the holder, the container

What is inside varies
It can be solid
It can be soft
It can be half filled
It can be overflowing

A vessel
That is what the body is for us
What is inside our vessel is for us to value and protect
Although we aren't responsible for which vessel we were given,
We should be responsible for what we chose to fill ours with

Are You Prepared To Meet The Doctor?

Whenever you have a scheduled appointment, it is very important to arrive prepared. If you rely on your memory at a time like this, you will most likely be disappointed with yourself later. It is so easy to think you know what you want to cover, get involved with conversation and end up leaving never addressing all of what you meant to. To alleviate this frustration and recognizing how terribly busy doctors are, I encourage you to always arrive with a list of what you need to address, to be sure it is all covered in that short appointment. Lists are simple but priceless when it comes to accomplishing all you need to during your visit. I start my list a few days before the appointment and make sure it is packed with my belongings the night before. You will find that when you come prepared, doctors tend to respect this and are happy to answer your questions. Believe me, it is a lot easier to come prepared than to walk out the door and then suddenly remember what else you meant to discuss. So, are you prepared to meet your doctor today?

Things to think to include in your preparation:

- A list of all current medications and their doses
- Your insurance cards
- Any questions you want to ask
- Reasons you are at this appointment
- Any test results
- A copy of your pharmacy phone number
- A list of any procedures and/or surgeries
- A list of any reactions to medications/foods
- A list of future goals to address

Pain Relief Brings More Advocacy And Quality Of Life!

In this chapter, I will be sharing methods I have used to achieve a better quality life with more purpose. I love what I heard Penney Cowan, founder & CEO American Chronic Pain Association, described in a lecture in DC, for a briefing for The Silver Book: Persistent Pain book release, February 20, 2013. She mentioned that we must get our tires repaired but then we have to be responsible to keep our tires maintained! So, below are the ways I keep my tires safe and inflated. All these topics mention take time and commitment. However, through trial and error, you need to find what it is that you can do daily to keep yourself as functional and as pain controlled as possible. When you can take the edge off your pain, then you have a chance for your life to be given back to you. For me, it has meant a chance to get very involved with advocacy work.

Medical Marijuana – My Form Of Pain Relief

Many of you are able to just go to a pharmacy and purchase the needed medication to help with your pain. For me, an aspirin, Tylenol and all the opiates are all out among many other choices. I had to live through each of these reactions, caused by my medical condition of EDS. Eventually, I was asked to try the new DNA Drug Sensitivity testing to see if there was any drug we had not tried that might help me. The test, covered by insurance, confirmed that all these reactions were REAL and I had a serious issue with metabolizing medication. In RI, it was finally suggested in 2007, that I try medical marijuana. I, at that point, was getting no quality sleep as I was attempting to still cope with two incurable, painful conditions while teaching. At the age of 57, this assignment brought on stress for I had tried marijuana socially my senior year in college and hated it. I ended up in bed for the remainder of the day feeling the sensation of being out of control of my body.

Despite numerous concerns, I tried some medical marijuana in an oil form, since smoking anything with sarcoidosis in the chest would be fatal. I realized immediately that I was destined to advocate for the only medication that allowed me sleep and pain relief. This medication, despite the controversy, was what was keeping me alive! How could I not speak out and let others know the gentle sensation you feel, that no one died from overdosing, and no one ends up with organ damage. And what was amazing is that now, living with a body in pain, I did not have a negative reaction to using it like I had had in college. I JUST GOT PAIN RELIEF! Back in the college days, my healthier body hated marijuana in the body and I spent the day in bed after just two hits! But now living in a body with pain, the reaction is different. A body in pain just gets pain relief using medical marijuana. There is no "high" or feeling "stoned", provided you do not use too much, so we need to educate others to understanding this!

Today, Stu and I have now dedicated ourselves to the legal use of medical marijuana. Along with speaking out nationally, we frequently get calls from doctors, nurses, physical therapists and others from our state and others, to help educate the next person in need of help. Many people we have met are just like I was, desperate for pain relief, yet afraid to try and use it due to the bad press out there.

PT – Manual Therapy

Another very important part of my life is the discovery of the benefits of manual therapy. It is important with this condition, to keep yourself aligned. It is a wonderful way for pain relief. I was originally fortunate enough to find two physical therapists that took the time to learn about Ehlers-Danlos. Thanks to their interest in "thinking out of the box", we quickly began to see the advantages of this type of physical therapy. I had had normal PT in the past where I had actually torn both my knees during appointments, despite the care of a wonderful physical therapist. Mind you, I was only pushing on a few pounds of weights on a machine, but that was all it took and we actually heard the tearing happen both times. The problem with this condition is that it is not good for our joints to jump right into lifting weights and working on machines unless we have been properly aligned and have strengthened the muscles. And even then, we are restricted on using no more than five lbs of weights or it stretches the ligaments and tendons even more, causing more subluxations and pain. With regular PT's , there is a lot of focus on weights and stretching, which is wonderful. But, a manual therapist aligns first and then begins the process of strengthening of the muscles in the body. This makes more sense to put the body in position and then strengthen! So, if you live with EDS, find yourself a good manual therapist that will learn to work with you and this condition and you, too, will begin to understand the pain relief that will come with these appointments.

Here in Rhode Island, we have now grown to more than just those two original physical therapists taking an interest. Both Mike and Trish at Healy Physical Therapy and Kevin and Linda at Muldowney Physical Therapy are skilled with helping us. In fact, **Kevin Muldowney** just recently wrote and launched his book called: ***Living Life to the Fullest With Ehlers-Danlos Syndrome.*** He was so concerned watching the number of us suffering and not moving forward, that he studied us and the condition, to figure out how we could strengthen our muscles without damage. Also, it bothered him thinking of the number of patients with Ehlers-Danlos from around the world that had no one to safely turn to for help. So, he worked to create a book that can be used with your **manual** physical therapist to get the safe treatment needed. The exercise protocol takes time and commitment, but if followed, in time you strengthen the specific muscles to help prevent frequent subluxations caused by the muscles in spasm. Then you are able to regain some control back on your life! I will be eternally grateful for his efforts, for this actually gives us all a chance to become stronger, safer, and eventually get better quality of life. Also, I have found that better understanding of this condition is beneficial.

Exercise

Along with a good physical therapy session, it is also imperative that you stay strong. Your ligaments and tendons are compromised with EDS, they are like overstretched rubber bands, getting looser as we age. So, your muscles are expected to pick up the job of their own and that of the ligaments and tendons. Being on constant overload, it is important to keep your core as strong as possible. A good exercise program is imperative to try to help yourself. If you choose to sit around and give in to this condition, believe me, that wheelchair will be your future along with allowing even more pain into your body. This is something you can have control of – go for it!

I walked, when my legs first allowed it. Today, after too many surgeries and four years in a wheelchair, I do walk, but may never be able to go long distances again. I have to get hoyered into the water since stairs are presently not an option for me. I use to jog with a belt around my waist and do leg exercises in the shallow end of the pool until that started to sublux the legs. So, I now kick on my back, not using my arms or neck and then turn over and kick on my stomach using a snorkel. On days I don't go to the pool, I ride a stationary bike, slowly increasing my distance and intensity. All days, I also spend time on the bed doing my core exercises. This all takes time, but it is my process to then have as good of a day as possible.

Weight Control

Those reading this that have EDS need to think about your weight! You are already compromised with weak tendons and ligaments along with your muscles on overload. So, imagine adding too much body weight to your frame! You really need to work with your diet, keep the weight down, and give your joints the best chance to be able to hold in position. Obviously, the more weight you carry, the more work your body will have. Controlling your weight is one more way to help control your pain!

Diet

If you are feeling sluggish, get frequent gas throughout the day and have a foggy head, then you may want to consider that you are dealing either with having food allergies, have candida or you are just not eating healthy foods. To help determine what the food triggers are in your body, you may want to visit a good dietician and have a blood tests done that specifies what foods are not being metabolized in your body correctly and thus are causing inflammation. If you do not address this, you are actually adding to the process of subluxing even more than necessary since inflammation in an EDS body means even more slipping out of position.

You will be shocked how much clearer your head will be and how much energetic you will feel when you eat more wisely. After years of issues, a doctor in Atlanta finally put me through a blood test series that was able to determine what my culprits were. Today, we have to eat around my many reactions that I have to dairy, soy, gluten, and the nightshade vegetables (potatoes, green peppers, tomatoes and eggplants) The best way I have found to handle this is to start my cooking from scratch. I have found that you can't go too wrong when you are creating a meal with organic, nutritious ingredients. We cut the cost down by growing a large organic garden each summer and then putting up as much as we can. Some items like applesauce, preserves and tomatoes we can, but the rest are stored in vacuum-sealed packages into the freezer. We are able to store in the cellar our supply of onions, potatoes, sweet potatoes and winter squash. Since cutting is a serious problem for me now with the progression of my condition, I have found that by taking my summer squash and roasting it first, I am able to manipulate the pulp into the blender, when cooled and puree it. This then gets frozen for winter soups. We have a meal of good soups weekly and consider it to be one of our favorite meals.

Small meals and snacks between the meals are a good route to go, but remember to be careful on the quantity and quality of food you are taking in. It was also researched and found that the largest meal should be before three PM, so keep the dinner meal smaller, if possible.

Positive Attitude – Making A Difference

Ehlers-Danlos is a lonely, misunderstood condition, to say the least. You have to fight with your emotions – throw away the "why me?" as quickly as you can. Who knows why us, but it is the life we have been given. Working to achieve a positive attitude in life goes a long way to make you happier, and thus your pain levels more tolerable. I have found that reaching out to others goes a long way to helping me, too. Once you begin this journey, you will find there is no turning back. As you turn your focus away from your troubles and instead turn to helping your fellow man, you will reap the benefits. You need to live with meaning and purpose and this attitude change will help a lot! We may be broken, but we can still matter and make a mark in life. So, go out there and make a difference. You will find by living life with a positive attitude, despite the pain and losses in life, you will find you will still like YOU.

My husband and I are constantly volunteering to advocate, testify for a cause we believe in, and opening our home to others seeking direction on how to cope with this tough diagnoses or those just living in pain due to other conditions. We are presently Ambassadors for the US Pain Foundation and Arthritis Foundation, on the board for RIPAC, RI Patient Advocacy Coalition, along with working to support marriage equality. We also have taken on the role of being caretakers for the medical marijuana program in our state. We presently grow and provide medication for ten patients between the two of us. These are just some of the things we do. We help them and in turn, this helps us!! And again, keeping busy with your mind and having purpose, all helps with pain relief!

Vecttor Treatment

After reading a book called, No, It's NOT in My Head, by Nicole Hemmenway, I just had to contact her and learn more about her successful treatment called the Vecttor Treatment. This machine was invented by Dr Rhodes in Corpus Christi, Tx. He invented this in attempts to stop the RSD pain brought on from surgery with one of his patients. He was determined to find a way to help her.

Nicole, who began to suffer terribly at the age of seventeen from RSD also, was referred to him after almost seven years with no relief and a deteriorating life. We had the pleasure of meeting her in person in NYC for the opening event of the traveling Invisible Project, in which I was the subject in story and photography for Ehlers-Danlos. Nicole handed each of us a signed copy of her book. It was a book I just couldn't put down. I just couldn't believe this horror story was hers for what we observed was a vibrant, motivated, beautiful now married woman. If you could see her today, you would not believe the transformation!

After reading the book, I quickly called her to get more information about the treatment she was using and to learn about Dr Rhodes. I was given his cell number and told to try calling him to discuss if this treatment could do anything to help EDS. After two conversations with him, we booked a trip down two weeks later.

In his office, he first checks your circulation to be sure you are not dealing with any blockage. As soon as that is ruled out, you then receive your first treatment. Like a tens unit, you put electrodes in a specific location given to you, and then the machine runs a slow current into your body. You treat the lower body first and then the upper body, each for forty minutes. What is happening is a slow current in working in the body to calm the system and help allow your body to help itself. As a guinea pig being the first EDS patient trying this, we had no idea what to expect.

What happen was immediate! That night, I was suddenly feeling like I had too much pain medication in my system! I immediately had to decrease from at that time four teaspoons of my oil to only one! Within one month, I had finally put needed weight on. I had been staying at 96 lbs no matter how hard I tried to gain. This was such a needed improvement to my life. The other thing I noticed in three months was huge – I no longer needed my blood pressure medication I was having to take to try to keep my blood pressure around 100/50, and that was a good day. Most of us with EDS have to deal with POTS, which means when we stand up, we either pass out or tend to get very dizziness. I became free of medication for a number of years and lived with NORMAL blood pressure thanks to Dr Rhodes and his Vecttor Treatment. A year ago, that changed due to the deterioration of the neck, so taking midodrine became necessary to keep the pressure back up.

If you decide to check into this, just understand that you make a commitment to this treatment for life. But if you feel the way I did, believe that is not a hard assignment to take on. I wouldn't miss my treatment for anything, for this is one more success story for helping me with controlling pain.

Prolotherapy

Most people I mention this to have no idea what this is! Prolotherapy involves the injection of an irritant solution into a joint space, weakened ligament or tendon insertion to relieve pain. Usually, a dextrose (sugar) solution is used along with lidocaine (a commonly used local anesthetic). The injection is administered at joints or at the tendons where they connect to the bone. These treatments are generally given every two to six weeks for several months.

I have tried prolotherapy for numerous parts of the body. Although it sounds scary and painful, it really isn't that bad. Back when I was still teaching, I always was back in the classroom the next day. I have had amazing success with the shoulder, elbow and the back and front of the neck. The biggest success has so far been with the neck. By the Spring of 2012, I was no longer able to hold a book and read for the dizziness and nausea became too intense. After just one of the four sessions, I was able to lie in bed, holding my kindle, and be able to read again. It was such a huge gain! So far, it looks like my elbow is now holding after many months of it constantly subluxing! Keep in mind that not all attempts are successful, but when they are, this can mean not having to turn to surgery for stability and pain relief! But remember, if you want to try this procedure, be sure to research out who you are going to for you need someone with exceptional experience.

Secret

Some of you will find this next section a little hard to swallow, and so did I when the suggestion first came to me. I was encouraged one day to sit and watch the video the Secret. Taking on my friend's suggestion, I began to check it out and found they quickly got into talking about putting out to the universe what it is you want and how to achieve it through the use of positive thinking. What was getting turning me off was when they were referring to those of us that want more money in life. I truly only want enough money to cover our bills. I have never had an interest in being materialistic. But, since I was on my stationary bike working out, I was stuck having to keep listening. As time went by, there was a message there for me that I believed was worth listening to. This was what they kept teaching – **you bring into your life what you think about.** Now I had to dismiss that I was responsible for bringing EDS into my body for I was born with that and had no influence in utero! However, I did hear their message that what you think about, you bring about. The video suggested making a list of things you want to have in life and each day, start your day looking at that list and thinking as of those things as becoming a reality. They also suggest that you begin the day being grateful for the good you do have in your life. Instead of saying this could never be and adding the negative to your thinking, say I look forward to this in my life.

So, I decided to take on this challenge. I typed out my list of things I wanted to change in my life and decided to focus on something that was very painful for me – eating away our finances with being disabled and having to leave my career of teaching prematurely. Each day, I would tell myself that I looked forward to having enough money to pay our bills – I wasn't asking to win the lottery, but wanted to get this monkey off my back of feeling responsible for jolting our finances by not being able to work. The video explains that you are not to worry about how this will happen, but to just believe it will happen. When I started this process, we were drowning financially. The stress it caused me was not healthy. If there was a crack to fall through, I had found it! I was officially declared disabled with no problem, but unable to collect social security disability since the last ten years of teaching, the town did not pay into social security. Upon my death, my husband will collect $1200 monthly from the town, in place of social security, but there was nothing for me to draw from while alive in place of not paying into social security. This felt so unfair, for I had paid into the system since the age of fifteen. It was only this last employment that didn't pay into the system but that didn't matter. The rule states that they look at your last ten years and if you worked those years and did not pay in, then you received nothing. Add to this that if my husband passed before me, then I also would not get half of his social security either, despite being disabled and unable to work. This was again because I HAD worked those ten years and not paid into the system. Nice reward for working and not sitting on my butt. I had to take any teaching job that came my way for they were very competitive! On top of this, I clearly was not going to be able at this point to be able to depend on my health to allow any commitment to employment.

So, this was my biggest stressor to face at this time. So, I was more than happy to see if this "positive attitude" could work with this situation. I have to admit that within a few months, realized that things financially just seemed to fall in place. Surprises would arrive, like the help we got from a gift made in my name for housing in WI for my surgery, unexpected checks arrived and we also learned to become successful growers of medical marijuana, take on patients and were able to get compensated for our expenses. Although we charge a small amount, it made a huge difference for us for before that, we had to absorb the cost to grow for only me. So, I have to say, today I have let go of the stress of having enough money and somehow, things keep seeming to fall in place and I actually don't dwell on finances anymore, which is good, for it really is the least of my problems to face with these major health issues!

Sex

Yes, sex is an important topic to be included. And what you want to know – the answer is YES, we have not given up on sex. No matter how tough life is becoming, try to not throw in the towel and give up on things that still matter to you due to pain. For us, sex is something we still value and have had to become creative to continue and keep me safe. Positioning with Ehlers-Danlos is the key. You need to find a position that does not cause more subluxations. For us, the solution is for me to be flat on the bed only. No, not the most exciting position to only use, yet we are able to have pleasurable relations and maintain our personal, sexual part of our relationship. To be honest, I have to not let my mind wander back to how things were, for it gets sad to remember what the past was like. However, I have no intention to let this part of my life go unless we have done all we can to hold on to it.

So living with pain? Don't just throw an important part of your relationship away without first discussing and considering if there are ways to still have this intimacy without doing damage to you. Remember, if you can get the edge off your pain, you will be able to succeed in doing things you thought you had said goodbye to!

Judgment – Happy Birthday To You!

You Look Great

10/22/06

You look great!
Oh no, not this again
You look healthy
Please, don't you understand?
Wow, how much are you exercising?
You have no idea

How do you make others understand?
We look normal
We have spirit
We care
We love life
We have dreams
We love solutions

But, the truth is
We struggle every day
We tread the waters to try to remain calm and productive

We don't know where to turn except to each other
We want to be brave
We don't want to bring others down
We don't have answers
We are scared of the future
We don't want sympathy,
We want respect and understanding

But the truth is,
We are living the hidden disability
It won't go away, but will progress
The pain won't stop, but it will increase
It won't allow us physical freedom, but will cripple us

You look great!
Thanks, I appreciate that
You look healthy
Thanks for the compliment

I guess we should be happy we look good to all of you
I guess the rest remains hidden
If only you wanted to know the real truth
But, what would we gain by telling you!

Judgment by others is so painful and so unnecessary, but so many of us experience this. This has affected all whelms of my life but probably the most painful first came from my long distance family that didn't see me often. Due to a smile on my face, I assume the assumption was that all was just fine. If I whined about what we are coping with, I would have been considered weak. So I choose to keep a lot of our daily struggles between me and my husband. Those living near us were seeing the ups and downs. Others living far enough away, did not see the daily struggle that we were dealing with. So, cards, flowers, and calls were rare. I had to talk with myself to remove the pain and hurt from this. You somehow assume those that grow up with you and love you, to also support you and not judge you, but that is not always the case. What felt like lack of support, from them not asking about what were are facing, was probably initially more painful than the doctors that also were judging me. Wasn't it enough that my life would never be able to return back to my normal again, without having to cope with judgment by those that are family and my need for their support? With my parents deceased, I always had it in my heart that at least family would be there to help support us with this difficult life that seemed to be robbing me of normalcy, but instead, at times, they could create the most difficult pain to try to cope with. I know I am loved but why did I feel like I was being judged or my issues were not worth discussing with me? I was lost how to handle the confusion and what felt like a lack of their interest, at times.

This has slowly improved, but at times I have to talk to myself when these moments get overwhelming so I can try to put life back in perspective. I get mad at myself for feeling so vulnerable and emotionally weak. Why I allow myself to get emotionally smothered by what I perceive as someone else's lack of empathy, is beyond me, but a fault for sure. I try so hard to keep a smile on my face, not wallow in the "why me" mode, find purpose in my life despite the constant pain and slipping backwards. And yet, there are people whose attitudes just crawls under my skin and festers inside of me. I am not proud of this part of my life – allowing myself to feel that judgment and get so hurt.

Two stories really stand out that topped all others. The first was a special birthday present shortly after being diagnosed with EDS. I was out of state with my husband, for what would be the last visit to see my parents alive. I was out for a walk with my husband, Stu, when a relative drove past us, stopped the car, and excitingly rolled down the window to share that they were giving me an early birthday present the next day. I would have an appointment, paid by them, to see a doctor, that was going to "make me all better". Stu and I were so excited to think we were visiting and a doctor away from home, knew how to help this condition. The next day arrived and off we went to the hospital. A very nice doctor greeted me at the door and we proceeded to talk for almost an hour. I could tell that things were in the winding down mode when I finally asked him what type of doctor he was, for he never requested to examine me. His answer, to this day, shocked me as he told me that he was a psychiatrist. This was my birthday present – happy birthday, Ellen – this sure felt like one more dose of judgment that had to be absorbed. I chose to never confront my family member about why I was sent to this appointment, for fear that this could actually undo our ties for good. I knew they loved me, I assume meant well and I did not

44

want to lose them. So, Stu and I ended up deciding to hold this hurt and confusion of this gesture inside of us, instead. But it did fester in us both.

The second example that comes right to mind was when I was sent to Dr Donut, a pulmonologist of the year in RI, for a second opinion. I was asked to go through testing to try to get to the bottom as to why I have episodes when the breathing gets cut off. I breathed through a tube while sitting up and then in a supine position, with a clothespin over the nose. Shortly after the testing, I was asked to go into the doctor's office. He wanted to talk with me for it seems that the test results did not come out like anyone he had treated before. My oxygen levels had dropped from 100% sitting up down to 69% while lying down. Because these results were out of the box, **I was asked if I had taken the test seriously!** I was taking three hours of my husband's time to get me there, paid a $25. Co-pay and was the one living with episodes of not breathing to the point that my service dog had to wake me up and bring me back. So, let's see, did I take this test seriously? How insulting can one get?

Playing Pretend   7/18/07

When I am around you
I am good at playing pretend
Living with EDS has taught me that
After so many years of not being diagnosed and understood
There was no choice but to put up my armor

I try not to tell you that I am scared
I try not to share the level of pain I have gained
I try not to explain how rapidly I feel this decline
I try not to tell you that I wonder how many more procedures this
body can take
Or how many more years I can endure this
I try to suck it all up and smile like all is well

However, a few of you allow me to let my guard down
You ask
You listen
I feel your compassion
You give me support and strength to move on
I thank you for that
For,
I prefer not to play the game of pretend!

Where Are My Friends?
I'm Not Dead Yet!

Being disabled makes your life smaller. You aren't able to get out into your normal social circles. Many of us lose our careers, which has provided a wide range of connections. Many times we are at the mercy of others transporting us around which is not conducive to spontaneity in life! Is there anything we can take away from this in a positive way?

I have learned so much with learning to live with these conditions. I have found some friendships get even stronger while others just fade away like they never existed. The most important thing I have gained from this is that it is important to be there when someone needs you, no matter what the inconvenience may bring to your day. When you are facing a situation in your life that seems to possibly bring you closer to your time on this earth, I find that some want to get even closer to you like you might hold some magic formula on how to handle it. And then, there are others you always considered dear friends that seem to just drift away from you. This is a painful experience. Here you are facing life coming to a quicker closing and also having to face the loss of friends. I have to wonder what they gain by slipping away? For me, it hurts not understanding why my unfortunate conditions turn some away. It is so important to prevent as much added stress as possible to try to cope and stay well – but this situation certainly adds confusion, loss and sadness on top of what has to be accepted, fought and lived in a positive manner. Why should those of us facing a possibly earlier death, forever pain, have to also feel like we are thrown out with the dirty water bucket too? Friends, I am not dead yet and would have loved to still have you in my corner that seems to be getting more and more hollow and scarce in numbers.

Last To Understand   11/06/06

Someone has to be last
If there's a first place, then there is a last place
By why would the people that can support me the most come in last
place?

Diagnosed with chronic illness
People near me daily see the recline
People near me share the sadness of loss
People near me encourage bright and hopeful solutions

But those so dear, yet so far away,
Why are they last to understand?

Maybe accepting I have a progressive condition is too painful to them
Maybe by convincing them and me that I can overcome this is helpful
Maybe talking about other things and not letting me speak out will
make this go away
Maybe they think I just don't suck it up enough and am weak

Why are they the last to understand?
They are the ones I need the most in my corner

I Needed...   12/05/06

I needed you
I needed you to not chew me up and spit me out
I needed you to be compassionate
I needed you to take time to ask and listen
I needed you to not judge this disease and me
I needed to feel your support

I needed your unconditional love
I needed you to boost me up when things got overwhelming
*I needed you to **lie** to me and tell me things would be okay*
*But I needed you to understand that this condition was **progressing***
rapidly** and **would not get better

I needed you to know how hard I was trying to cope
I needed you to express pride in me as I searched for answers, educated
myself and
*   Kept a smile on my face despite all my losses*
I needed you to take just a moment in my shoes and try to understand

But most of all,
I just needed you,
I get frightened
I wonder what the future has left for me
Why weren't you able to be there for me?
I just needed you to help me get through this

Despite the disappointments of friends that have chosen to drift away, the following people in our lives have stood out to truly be there for us with compassion. The following have remained strong in our lives. I would like to share a few of these friends with you so you can understand what a true friend can mean in life:

Pam — Weekly Check In/Visits

There is one friend I never have to question about my relationship with. Pam Fracareta and I have known each other since one of our sons attended her cozy day care at her home in Foster, RI. Pam and her family built a home from an old one-room schoolhouse! Later on in years, we both ended up being hired in Burrillville, RI, to teach at the middle school. Pam and I made a sincere effort to meet for morning coffee on the way to school as close to a weekly basis as we could adhere to. After about ten years, I transferred to Pam's eighth-grade team to teach Social Studies. The funny part was here we were now working together, but actually found less and less time to meet to just socialize. Topics seemed to be more about our team of approximately a hundred twenty five students.

Since I retired, Pam has made an amazing effort to try to visit weekly. For many years, it was on a Tuesday, after her piano lesson, that she would stop in. I would always laugh about this day selected for I use to read "Tuesday With Morrie" with my students during our sociology unit. So, I began to call this visit my "Tuesday's with Pam"! Presently, Pam now has taken on a few teaching positions in local colleges so we now try to meet on Fridays. She is such a sincere friend that shares her life with me and makes me feel loved and cared for. I remain so grateful for her friendship. She asks how I am and cares to listen if I need to share the truth - she is an example of how demonstrating through her actions the simple and priceless act of caring for others.

Karin And Lucky

Never did I realize that when I signed on to become the proud owner of a service dog, that this would change my life forever with new friendships too! Karin, Wendy, Eddie and I all met in November of 2009, when matched with our service dogs. Karin and I were placed in rooms in one area of the house and Eddie and Wendy on the other side. Due to this, we developed special relationships with our roommates.

How does one deal with so much hardship is just beyond me, but Karin has for years? It began with growing up in Sweden, being adopted to a wonderful family that also adopted a brother that is the most amazing sibling one could ask for. And then the horror develops – being raped as a teen while in a horse stall cleaning for her employment, her family moving to the states, attending college, being raped again, developing type I diabetes, gets married, being diagnosed with ovarian cancer, making the courageous decision as a young woman to delay treatment to get pregnant in hopes of having at least one child before her chances will be gone with treatment, giving birth to a beautiful baby girl, leaving her new baby one day in the morning with her parents to do chores to only being hit sitting at a light in the back by a drunken twelve year old that has stolen his parents car – all leading to eleven months in a body cast in the hospital, this leads to her husband leaving them for this is too much for him to handle, she opens her heart and home to at least seventeen foster teens, but as time progresses, Karin's health continues to deteriorate with other bouts of cancer, severe back pain to cope with from the car accident, and a life that constantly seems to get thrown upside down and just recently, adding MS to the list of conditions to cope with. And yet,..........this woman has courage, determination and spirit that can light a room and make us all feel minute when observing what she daily has to cope with. This special woman became my friend that I will always be grateful to have in my life for we can laugh, cry and help each other cope with the uncertainty that life seems to bring us due to our health issues.

West Allis Hospital Staff

Another example of people reaching and helping out happens each time we have had to travel from our home in RI to WI for my surgeries. The staff at the West Allis Hospital have consistently gone out of their way to make us feel welcome and at home. They set up a medical plan for us, including getting an electric wheelchair to use so I can help take care of Maggie the service dog. They also create a volunteer list of people to help me get her outside until I am well enough to take over. The head dietician emails me before arriving to check on any new food issues and then actually comes up to the room to check in with me and work on the weekly menu. I have had them even asking me if I wanted to have Reiki during and after the surgery to give this body the best chance for a successful surgery and recovery. And, essential oils have been used to help me with pain and congestion. I never regret returning to this hospital for they make us feel like they are our family away from home. It is always such a pleasure to return to see them but just once, it would be such a treat if it was just for a visit, and not more surgery! They have become very meaningful friends to us and we are grateful!

You Stand Out   12/17/06

For over 23 years, I have walked down the same road
Why is it that today I suddenly noticed you standing out?
There you were, tall, straight and different from the others
All the other trees had curves and bends, seeming to try to reach to the sky
But not you, you were strong and bold and seemed to know the direction to grow
How did you accomplish that?
You stood out.

It stayed on my mind for a week about noticing this tree.
Why would that make such an impression on me?
And then the connection to life came to me
There are certain people in my life that stand out
They are compassionate, dedicated, and unique
They are the ones we wish we could emulate
They are my heroes and examples in life

They stand out
They touch many and ask for little in return
They are what I refer to as being the salt of the earth
How does this happen to them?
Why is it that these few just seem to fall into these positive roles of leadership?
What a world this would be if we could learn how to all achieve this level in life.

Acts Of Kindness

I have had some amazing experiences with new and unexpected friendships and acts of kindness to share with you. We have experienced feel good stories that were not anticipated, so the memories of them remain strong.

John — NEADS

After an eight-month wait after my interview for a service dog, I got antsy one day when we drove down to the beach for a day adventure. In the car on the way back home, I decided to call NEADS to see if there was a dog in the wings being prepared to match with me. I was ready for months for this help and companionship. The trainer took my call and kept asking me if I had gotten their call today. I kept saying, that no, I am calling you. We went back and forth like this until he finally got that no one had called and he was stunned, for on his list of things to do that specific day was to call me and tell me I was being matched with another black lab whose name was Magpie! I had two weeks to get life in order, figure out how to arrive there with both my scooter and wheelchair. We had no idea how we would accomplish getting these items up there until one day the doorbell rang and there was John, one of Stu's old high school classmates. Suddenly hearing our predicament, he immediately offered his services to not only get all equipment up there but also offering to return and bring it back two weeks later. What was the chance that this person from the past would end up passing our house and deciding to stop in and say hello after seeing an article about us in the paper. John was a gift that seems to come out of nowhere – suddenly at our doorstep at the right moment. We will always remember this act of kindness and love sharing the story!

Jeff Wolfson – Kathy's House

Traveling to WI became a yearly adventure for me to find help to secure and stabilize these loose joints surgically. Despite many doctor visits throughout this area, we have not succeeded in finding any doctor willing to take the time to learn how to help me, so this has been my only answer for the past eight years. Traveling out of state means a huge financial burden for us – the cost of flying, accommodations for two weeks, paying a person to live on the farm to tend to the animals and plants, etc. Along with this comes the issue of also leaving your support group – no family or friends to visit you or turn to! Twice, we have arrived to Kathy's House in West Allis, WI, checked in and been told that we don't owe any money because there had been a donation made in our name. It turned out to be an old high school classmate from Livingston, NJ, Jeff Wolfson, who decided to surprise us and make this donation. His wife had had serious environmental allergies that were life changing to their family. She, after many years, did improve and get back into life but they never forgot what it was like to have health issues turn your life upside down. Jeff left his career while his wife was suffering and opened a health store instead and developed a deep interest in people and compassion to all types of struggles. Jeff and I were never close friends in high school, yet he and his wife twice decided to help us out and pay it forward. How do you begin to thank people so generous like this? We try to pay if forward and find a way to try to help others out in any way possible.

Dog Blanket Gift

One example was in the winter of 2013, a woman approached me in our local Whole Foods and wanted to talk about Maggie, my service dog. Within only a few minutes, she told us that she wanted to give us a present, for she was a seamstress and has a business making dog blankets for the car. We parted sharing email addresses and I was shocked to hear back from her the next day. We met a week later and presented us with a gorgeous dog blanket that we travel proudly with.

Maggie, my service dog, absolutely love her new blanket. She seems secure, cozy and always very happy to settle in for a trip. I would highly encourage any dog owner to consider this wonderful addition to keeping your car clean while your dog feel so loved!

Physical Therapy

As time progressed with my condition, I found myself going to Pt weekly. The results are amazing, but the cost becomes huge having to foot the bill for a co-pay. My physical therapist, at the time, Mike Healy, owner of Healy Physical Therapy, suggested I fill out a form in his office to see if I would qualify for a reduction of the co-pay. After turning the form in, I was told at the next appointment that I would no longer have to pay the copay due to my financial situation. I wonder sometimes if they just didn't quietly just change the rules to help me out. To not have to come up with a fifteen dollar co-pay is such a huge help considering I attend presently PT five days a week. At this point, three of the days are at Healy's for the cranial PT and the other two are at Muldowney PT to work with Kevin, who branched off with his own business after working at Healy's for a few years. Between these two amazing men, I have been kept safe and cared for. Eventually Trish was added to Healy's and Linda to Muldowney's, adding two more with magical hands of help and woman filled with compassion. I keep dreaming that we will be able to cut back, but with now over twenty-three surgeries to recover from, the need to attend never seems to be put to rest. It warms my heart to have these people in my corner. Entering their places of employment has truly become like visiting family. The staff is so kind and compassionate.

Dr Cummings And Liz Prinz

It's not a picnic to have to pack up, leave our farm, pets and life as we know it and travel to WI for surgeries. When we fly out there, it means for me, two weeks in the hospital and rehab unit until I am strong enough to be able to travel home. For my husband Stu, it means two weeks of added stress, none of our family around, and having to keep himself healthy emotionally and physically to deal with the time away.

There are a few things that make this whole process much more positive for us. First, it helps to be grateful to have an attentive and caring doctor, Dr Patrick Cummings, who, for whatever reason, has taken on this rare condition and figured out

60

ways to help stabilize the joints. Without him in my life, I would most likely not be back to some walking again after about four years in leg braces and use of the wheelchair. His former office manager, Liz Prinz is what I call my guardian angel. She was always upbeat, efficient and right on top of all the arrangements that need to be made to make this long distance event happen.

Neighbors – Pattie, Karen And Vinny

But back on the home front, we have also been blessed with amazing neighbors. Pattie and Karen have many times taken it upon themselves to keep the farm running and the property safe for the two weeks we are away. Pattie stayed in our home for two of my surgeries and Karen filled in to take out our other dog at lunch time, get food into the house for our return, and be the back-up for Patti, if she had a delay getting back home. To come home to clean house, ready for us to move back in has been such a huge gift. Also, Vinny, who for years lived across the street from us, went out of his way to help us in any way needed. Whether it is waking up to the driveway plowed, helping Stu carry something too heavy or just lending his expertise on how to do things on the farm, he has always been there. If only all of you could have neighbors like ours, what a kind world this would be!

Dan

September 2009, I was interviewed in RI for the Providence Journal, about medical marijuana. Not only did this front page article begin my openness to speak out, but it also exposed us to the world about growing. At that point, we were just trying to figure this process out. We were successful gardeners, but had never attempted growing marijuana. I had called the Department of Health and explained that we lived out in the country and asked if it was acceptable to grow in our garden outside. Unfortunately, the person that took my call did not give us the correct information by saying this was acceptable. Only inside growing or an attached area to the house was allowed. So, when I was photographed for the paper, a young man saw the photo and felt concerned for us. I received a facebook message from a person name Dan, who mentioned that we looked like we needed help and was he right. In time, with he offered to come over and help us set up inside. This amazing person took on the project to set up a safe growing set-up. Stu and I enjoyed this young man being around the house despite our years were far apart.

It turned out that Dan was also living a life as a disabled person. He had lived through the horrors of the Station Nightclub fire in our state. Although he didn't get burned, he was now emotionally scarred for life. No longer could he work and getting out of bed, yet alone out of the house was a daily challenge. Yet, here was this young man reaching out to us to give us aid.

We have remained connected to Dan through the years. We are worlds apart with our beliefs, yet this emotionally damaged man has been able to give to and accept us as we are. If only more people could have relationships where you could laugh at the differences instead of shying away. Thanks to Dan, we now are able to successfully grow medical marijuana for our limit of five patients each!

Shadows   11/27/06

Black, shades of gray
Still or moving
Shadows are part of many of our days

Why are they there?
Are they there to keep us from feeling alone?
Are they there to add more confusion to our lives by their overlapping
images?
Are they there for any purpose?

We notice that they are there on sunny days,
Yet, they cast their spells in dark shades
We notice they sometimes get ahead of us,
Thus feeling like they are alive

So, why are there shadows?
I would like to believe they represent all those that I need close to me
I would like to believe that they are my guardian angels
I would like to believe that on cloudy day, when they aren't able to
present themselves,
 that they are just taking a break to regain their strength.
I would like to believe that they are for me and you serving as guidance
and support in life.

How Do I Escape?

When one needs a breather from one you love, you can take a walk, go out for a ride around town, visit a friend or come up with other distractions that help you put life and the relationship back into perspective. So, what do you do when you can't walk and drive? I have moments that I want to scream and want to just step away – but how am I to accomplish this? These moments are so difficult for me. I am use to working out my issues for the most part by myself, but when my relationship needs a break that is getting harder to work out. I use to take advantage of long walks at the reservoir or swimming in a lake or pool before I became so disabled. And now here I am not able to make my exit from my own life. This will always be something I struggle with. Being so dependent is not fun, but not being able to be with yourself in a manner needed to calm life is a huge challenge.

When we need a break from each other, neither is happy. We function most of the time like a well-oiled machine, but we are human and sometimes it all gets just too overwhelming. If you can, take that walk, immerse yourself in something you love, call a friend, write, write, write. Any way you can express your emotions and release that stress will help you put the pieces into a better perspective.

My ways of distracting myself have had to be adjusted yearly as my condition worsens. In my healthier past, I turned to doing crafts, reading, gardening, walking, and a short excursion to the store, to now at times at a loss as to what to do. I love feeling productive, so it is a real challenge as your disability progresses, to find new outlets. Sometimes such simple things like calling a friend can help, baking a treat, cleaning out a cupboard, or jumping on a scooter and taking a ride down the street and getting some fresh air can lighten up life. Don't settle for sitting and doing nothing when you feel overwhelmed. Find something that makes you feel happy. It is hard to let those other options go, but you also can't continue to dwell on what you have lost in the past. This is your now and you need to value it and find new resources to turn to.

The Uninvited Guest   10/31/06

Who asked you to join me?
I didn't expect you and I don't wish to recognize you
Why did you choose to come to me?
And, when can I expect you to leave?

You are with me constantly
I feel you in my blood
I am drained by your presence
I am losing my life as I've know it
All because of you, the uninvited guest

So, when are you leaving?
No one seems to be able to help me get rid of you
This has gone on for too long
I hope you know you were not invited
Why can't you get the hint that you are not welcome?
You need to leave me
Let me have the quality of life return

You are an uninvited guest

Your Umbrella   11 / 2 / 06

With your umbrella,
You try to shield out rain, sun or even snow
With your umbrella,
You make that choice to not be touched by nature's gifts for that
moment

Not every day is successful with your umbrella
Some days, the wind blows too strong and you are forced to feel the
gusts
Some days, the rain is so strong that you still get drenched
And, some days, the umbrella is just not working at all
Then, you must deal with the onslaught of precipitation

I, too, have an umbrella
I actually try to use mine everyday
I, too, use it to shield my body
When it's working, it helps to shield me from the difficulties of life

But, as you have found out,
I am not always able to put my umbrella up
I try to find a way to repair mine
But if that doesn't work, I try to find a different umbrella
The worst that happens is I must live without my shield for that
moment

We need to treasure and protect our umbrellas
We find comfort in knowing they are there when we need them

68

But we also need to know it's okay to have moments without them
We can see it as a challenge,
We can learn to just roll with the punches and make the best of it.
Life can go on without our umbrellas

Snap, Crackle And Pop

Those of us living with Ehlers-Danlos, the ones that easily sublux due to lax ligaments and tendons would be great material for writing a horror flick! Whenever I try to describe to anyone about what happens in this body, I am looked at like I am nuts! Really? Your body can slip out of place with a simple hug, a wrong twist or picking up over five pounds? Yes, that's us! We snap, crackle and pop.

After my twenty-first surgery on my leg and spending five months non- weight bearing and having to live in a wheelchair, I was able to start walking again. Within just a few weeks, the new surgical leg decided to sublux, which had been the reason for surgery to correct this process. I lightened up the walking, had it repositioned, rested and then began to try again. The good news is I made it through the next two months with the right fibula staying in place while walking in the house. It seems that the muscles were getting stronger and holding the bone in position. However, just a few weeks ago, the left, good foot subluxed. That foot has already endured two major surgeries. So again, the emotions had to be put in check and I had to somehow try to remain positive that this would settle back down and hold again. Well, it has now been another two weeks, the foot is holding, but NOW the surgical leg decided to have the fibula sublux again, meaning a partial dislocation. This is the chaos you live with living with Ehlers Danlos. No matter how hard you try to stay on top of all this, we snap, crackle and pop all the time and most times without warning.

Suspended In Liquid   *11/1/06*

I twist, it snaps
I bend, it pops
I sit, it shifts
I walk, it rotates
I lay in bed and don't dare roll over
I am suspended in liquid

Your body has strong ligaments, tendons and muscles
My body is held together with muscles only
Your bone structure is strong and secure
Mine is suspended in liquid

I haven't given up
I work those muscles daily
But, I seem to be losing the battle

My joints sublux constantly
So many things I did before are gone forever
EDS has me suspended in liquid

let's

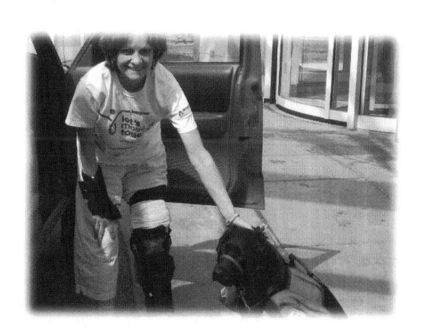

Service Dog – Take A Breath!

After meeting another woman in RI also living life with EDS, I got inspired when I met her service dog she had gotten from NEADS, Dogs for Deaf And Disabled Americans. I was at the point that we had lost our two dogs due to old age, so it was time to think about who would replace them. I decided to take her cue and try applying for a service dog too. I remember being taken to NEADS, in Princeton, Ma and being so nervous. I was so use to having to prove to others that there was a problem, but I quickly realized that wasn't necessary there. They had already interviewed others with this rare condition, so I had no worries about being approved. At first, there was thought that a dog named Basket would be assigned as my match. (When people donate $1000 to NEADS, they are given the chance to name a puppy, thus explaining the strange name!) We met at my interview and worked a little bit together; me in my wheelchair and her gently by my side. However, the call that was suppose to come in to me in two weeks never happened and my heart sunk. I finally called to find out why I wasn't hearing to learn that she did not pass the final test doing her assignments when other animals were around. Due to her getting distracted, she was demoted to being a therapy dog. Strangely enough, later when I did get matched, both dogs had the same graduation date and we were able to meet the little boy she was assigned to. He was autistic yet was able to take over the microphone and tell over four hundred quests that he loved his dog very, very, very.......much. There was not a dry eye in the audience. This dog recently had traveled to Disney and even rode the rides with his new match. Clearly, as the mother described, this young man was already gaining – for he had people coming up to him now to meet his dog, all helping him to learn to socialize.

So on to whom became my match!

The big day came eight months after the interview and I truly wondered how I would cope for two weeks without Stu's help. I was totally wheelchair bound at this point, not feeling very well and emotionally weak. But things were to change forever in my life not only getting a canine partner, but also gaining three new friends that also were being matched with their dogs. Eddie, from NJ, was being matched with Magpie's brother, a much larger yellow lab, Karen, was matched with Lucky, who eventually became my dog's best friend, and Wendy, who was matched with Allie (who within a year was discovered to be going blind and had to be returned and demoted as just a pet. Fortunately, there was a happy ending for all with this situation when her foster family volunteered to adopt her) Wendy, who found tremendous strength to get through this horrific situation that had never happened before with a service dog, was later matched again with a beautiful black lab named Tippy.

We worked our human tails off trying to catch up with these dogs and their commands and skills. The first week, I really wasn't sure I could get through this. Somehow, however, Maggie (I changed her name from Magpie to Maggie with their permission) and I began our bond as she patiently waiting as I gained my confidence and command of what I was to do as her match. We ended up having an amazing second week of training and even passed our final test!

Before I knew it, Maggie and I came home together to our new life of being partners. Six days after coming home, it was 4AM Thanksgiving morning, the house was filled with our four grown sons and two wives, and I was suddenly being woken up to licking and stimulation. It took me a long time to respond, so Maggie kept working on me. She had jumped onto the bed when she detected that I was in trouble with my breathing. It was tough to become more coherent, but when I did, I suddenly realized my new partner had just saved my life! She woke me up to get me back to breathing, and as I write this book, you can see that she succeeded! I have since been assigned to keep Maggie next to me on the bed at all times instead of taking any chance of her jumping and possibly landing on this body that would easily be damaged. So, thanks to Maggie, I keep taking that breath of life. I have told her that she can't leave this world before me!

ELLEN LENOX SMITH

If I Don't Wake Up   2/13/07

If I don't wake up
It will be okay
The sun will still shine
The rain will still fall
The seasons will keep changing
New designs and development will continue on

If I don't wake up
It will be okay
Life will continue on
The birds will still sing
The gardens will still bloom
Families will keep growing

If I don't wake up
It will be alright
I will leave you to continue to enjoy all the gifts of life
And you will enjoy them knowing that
I am now in peace, away from the daily pain
It will be all right.

How Am I? Ask My Cat! 5/25/08

People ask me, how are you?
I use to think I had some clue,
But my cat makes we wonder
She seems to be my new barometer to how I am

When I am well,
She climbs onto my chest
She licks my face
She stretches her paws out my neck and caresses me
She snuggles down into me and takes her nap
I lay there and stroke her silky long fur
I feel the sensation of her beating heart
I am content and loved

When things aren't as they should be in my chest
I no longer have this sweet visitor
She will avoid me
She will not want to climb on my chest
Days will pass until I have passed her health test

When she senses I am again okay,
Then she becomes my buddy
It is comforting to know I am okay on those days she wants to be near
It is terribly unsettling when she ignores me

So, ask my cat, not me, how I am!

Hospital Bed Transition

In June of 2007, my bilateral foot surgery was done to attempt to hold these feel together with cadaver tendons. The goal was to attempt to put weight on my feet again. This procedure required me to live with two casts for five months along with life in a wheelchair and being totally non-weight bearing. It was needed for me to sleep in a hospital bed to be able to manipulate with a transition board to either the wheelchair or commode. Life was tougher than ever at this time. We placed the hospital bed, that we thought was a temporary need, in our living room. I spent many long nights in that room looking forward to the day I could return to the bedroom and our queen bed.

It was as this time that my breathing issues began to develop. I suddenly one night, just before going to sleep, experienced a sensation as I was falling asleep of falling off a cliff and feeling the worse dizziness I had ever had. This came out of nowhere. We learned later that this was due to the fact that the day after the surgery, while being taught how to transition to the board, I had pushed too hard on my left arm, the side where in just seventeen months earlier I had had reconstruction of the sternoclavicular joint. I had actually torn out the tough procedure I had just healed from. This tearing caused the area to become loose.

I dreamed in my mind that this would just go away and life would become a bit more normal again, but instead, this continued to deteriorate, eventually leading to significant breathing issues. Now instead of the bone pushing out as it was before surgery, it was now pushing in, causing the sternum to shift down and the trachea to twist. Despite eventually graduating from a CPAP to a Bi-Pap ST Advanced machine that pushed air and out of the lungs, things just kept getting worse.

So, as my months progressed and I was finally able to return to these feet, a huge decision had to be addressed. Would I be able to safely return to my bed or would this now have to be my new life? A hospital bed has a huge advantage of being able to lift the head or feet up and down along with the actual height of the bed frame. Therefore, when I experience the pressure from the shifting trachea and or the sternum, the hospital bed allows me to play with positioning to try to breath better. It was a clear, but very emotional decision to swallow – if I wanted to have every chance to breath and keep me from episodes of breathing being cut off, I would have to remain for life in that hospital bed to sleep.

We lightened up this big decision by quickly removing our queen bed, bringing down the single bed our now grown sons used upstairs and placed that and my new hospital side by side in our bedroom and then threw a king size quilt over the two of them. It actually is amazing how normal it makes the bedroom looks and I go to bed each night being as safe as I know how to be. There are just circumstances like this that you have to be able to let go, accept the situation and move forward with the new life you are living. I rarely allow myself to think back as to how things use to be for it is hard to really imagine that so many changes have had to be made from the normalcy I have known. This is now the life I am living and I don't want to waste the time I have left being bitter and always let down – so hospital bed it is!

The Drifter   12/27/06

I use to be a doer
I use to be a fixer
But now,
I am a drifter.......

Gone are the plans I can count on
Gone are the dreams that will come to fruition
Gone is the career I thrived in
Because now I am a drifter

Life is still bustling around me
People are animated, busy and on the move
Their vacations are amazing
Their careers are blooming
All while I am a drifter

Like a breeze that passes by your face
Many joys of life are no longer possible
I need to accept this and continue to look for the good
For, I am drifting from the life I have loved and known
Life is still here for me
But now it is to be lived as the drifter

If it Can't Hurt You, Why Not Try?

I live with these difficult conditions with a motto – if it can't hurt, why not try? This allows me to be comfortable to search for and consider trying new ideas out there. Some things just didn't help me or eventually I realized were not safe like acupuncture for me, and conventional surgeries, but other things have made a dent in helping to provide better quality of life. I don't dream of a cure or this just disappearing from my life. However, I always dream of having better moments. I've turned to NIH to be involved in their research, tried turning to homeopathic medicine, various diet restrictions, braces, writing, music, joining a choir, finding my voice and advocating, testifying for things I believe strongly in, along with finding a surgeon that has learned how to help hold my joints together using cadaver tendons. The sky's the limit. Listen to others. Search out what they share with you and decide if it is worth a try. And don't be afraid to drop everything and try something that may help. In 2010, my husband and I literally did just that and within two weeks after a conversation with Dr Rhodes, flew to TX to try his Vecttor treatment. I was the first person with my conditions to try it and the results have been worth the time and money. Had I not taken that chance, I would still be taking blood pressure medication three times a day to try to keep my pressure from dropping below 100/50, or much lower. I knew that the treatment wouldn't hurt me, but could possibly help me and took that chance. So don't cut yourself short and assume there is nothing else to turn to! Keep your mind and ears open and remember, if it can't hurt you, give it a try – it may help you!

IV Or PICC Line

Many dealing with Ehlers-Danlos have issues eventually with having blood drawn and even holding an IV line. I went through many surgeries with the IV line put in, and then experiencing, usually IN the middle of the night, of the line falling out or just plain infiltrating. In fact, one night, a nurse came into the room to administer my pain medication into the line and I tried to explain that it was burning as it was being injected in. I was told that everything was "just fine" and I assumed I was just overreacting! Well, about an hour, I called for help for the pain levels had dramatically increased. This time, a new nurse walked into the room. When I shared that I thought the line was not in place, this nurse took more time to examine me and totally agreed with me. Thus, the medication had never gotten into the vein and the increase of the pain was real! They had to call for the ICU nurse to come down to try to get a new line in. Of course this all happened in the middle of the night, so sleep was not too successful that night or all the other nights that this kept happening to me.

So, it was time to consider the recommendations being made to me by the hospital staff to go for a PICC line for the next surgery. If this suggestion is made to you, go for it. I have never had the line slip out and have been able to make it through many nights with sleep and pain relief getting to the right location! Unfortunately, the magic does seem to be slipping with the success of this type of line for as the surgeries progress. I am now hearing how weak my vessels are and they are now implying that a central line is in order. Somehow, that just sounds like the end of the line for me so as they work to get the line in now having to use the ultrasound, I just keep asking them to try one more time, and so far, this has been the magic!

No CPR?

Imagine having to push on a chest that is so weak that if you get a hug, the ribs immediately shift and sublux! How could I possibly have CPR on this chest with Ehlers-Danlos? CPR requires significant pressure on the chest. A few years back, my thoracic doctor suggested that I put on my orders to not ever have CPR. Now that does sound like giving up with life when you add that to your requests. However, the doctor explained that I would not want to return to the life I would have to face if he had to reconstruct my chest after the damage that would be to the ribs and sternum.

I was totally understanding the circumstances and appreciated his honesty about this. But, a pulmonologist that I was sent to for another opinion, Dr Donut, called me into his office to question this decision and ask why I was giving up on my life at such a young age. Give up on life? Was he serious? I have dedicated my life, since this diagnoses, to find nothing but answers, direction and help. And here this doctor was joining in on the crusade of judgment that so many of us face, even when we finally get our diagnoses. What his comment told me was that he was not vested in understanding my condition. I was hurt, and then even questioned myself to the point of actually calling the thoracic doctor to share what had been said to me to hear his response. And guess what? He reiterated the same thing – I would not want to wake up to the reconstruction that would have to be done. So, the order remains and I will have to stay strong to keep these orders in place when others decide to judge me again someday!

Blocking Out

As my husband and I have discussed the reality of our life since realizing the severity of my diagnosis, we realize that we have literally blocked out so much of what we have had to endure. For instance, we have upstairs in my former bedroom, a room filled with all the braces I have had to use through the years for almost every body part. I have asked Stu to take them all to the calling hours when I pass and to put them on display to just give perspective to others as to what Stu has had to cope with, with me. We try to think back to the many trails we have had to endure and at times, it gets difficult to remember. By the way, I referred to the upstairs as my former bedroom since I have not been able to use stairs for a number of years due to the legs not cooperating and having surgery after surgery to try to remedy the issues of loose ligaments and tendons causing the bones to slip.

One particular surgery was something we try not to focus on for it was a crazy moment for us. In 2012, we went arrived in WI, for my twenty-first surgery to try to resolve the issues with my legs and lack of stability. The goal was to have bilateral surgery to take care of a minor problem on the left leg and major repair for the right leg to try to hold the fibula in place with cadaver tendons tunneled through the tibia. Leaving home for two weeks is not an easy task when you leave behind animals on the farm, a garden of medicine growing in the cellar, and friends and family for support. Stu has a routine when we get there. He is determined to eat well, exercises and visits twice a day for the two weeks I am in the hospital. But, all this clearly adds more stress to life.

Five days before leaving, Stu ended up with an ambulance ride to the hospital due to passing his fist kidney stone. At first, we had no idea what was wrong and both assumed the whole surgery was not going to happen. Fortunately, after passing the stone, he quickly rallied and we moved forward with the plans to travel to WI.

The journey to WI was to be a two-flight journey. When we first landed in Michigan, I had to wait on the plane for my wheelchair to be brought up from the plane storage area. When Stu opened up the chair for me to sit in, the entire seat fell through. Not only was the wheelchair broken, they had somehow managed to break a metal bar in half, and not even at a joint. So here we were stuck without a way to get me around and I was about to have surgery that was putting me into a wheelchair for over three months, totally non-weight bearing. Talk about adding stress! Although Delta kindly ordered a rental to be waiting for us when we landed in WI, it took four months to get my wheelchair replaced and working properly.

The day before the surgery, we were invited to lunch with a family that is also coping with Ehlers Danlos. As we drove towards the mall where we to meet, we started to notice helicopters in the sky that were just hovering in the air and thought it was strange. We then arrived to meet for lunch, just three miles from Kathy's House, where we were staying. To our shock, we were greeted by a locked down due to a spa shooting. Many police with machine guns greeted us and we heard of the horror of a mass shooting in the state that affected many that we met. For instance, my surgeon's daughter's hairdresser was one of the casualties and one of my nurses also lost her neighbor that stepped in front of a teen girl that was a target to protect her from her step father. He ended up shooting the woman and killing her as she saved the life of this young lady. The stories of connections to the lost continued during our stay in the state. It was a pretty horrific event, and here it was the day before major surgery when you try to keep positive! This sure didn't help!

The particular surgery went well, but from the moment I woke, up in the room, things just seemed out of control. Surgery began at 9:30AM but I didn't wake up until 4:30! I normally wake up in the recovery room, but the ketamine infusion they had given me knocked me out for hours. When I finally became coherent, they asked me if I wanted to be put into the ICU so I could be given more infusions to help with pain, explaining that you can't have them in a regular room. Mistake number one, I told them I would be fine using my oral ketamine. I had had the same surgical procedure on the other leg a few years back and thought I would be able to be on top of the pain. What ended up happening is that this surgery was much more extensive and for many more hours. Therefore, the oral medication was too weak and it was finally determined that I needed to take it not every four hours but instead hourly. I quickly realized I would not have enough medication I had had made by my compound pharmacist to get through the two weeks.

I made the call to RI to have more medication shipped to WI directly to the hospital, but something major was about to happen that would make this delivery impossible to be in time.

After a week in the hospital, I was shipped about forty minutes away to another hospital that had an inpatient rehab unit for another week so I could get strong enough for the long flight back home to RI. We arrived to a gorgeous new building and a wonderful staff that immediately began the intake. All was going well, despite my exhaustion until a young woman came into the room from billing. She proceeded to tell us that my Blue Cross coverage was not active for one month – including the time we were in WI for this surgery. Here we were getting this information on a late Friday afternoon and wondering what we were suppose to do. I had to ask them to stop the intake questions so we could take the time to call the insurance and my town that I had been previously employed with. To make a long story short, it turned out to be a total mistake, but the result of this initial news was significant stress added to an already tiring day of transition.

To our dismay and alarm, Hurricane Sandy had developed and was wreaking havoc along the east coast. We sat in my hospital room, out of touch with all we loved as this horrific storm made it way into all of our lives. Getting news about RI's condition was almost impossible since most coverage was about the more congested areas like NY and NJ. We had spoken to our four sons the night before it began and asked them to text when they could to report in. As it turned out, all four, did okay. The two in NYC were the lucky ones that kept their power, but they saw some very sad situations and almost felt guilty for doing as well as they did. One of the two sons was actually only two blocks from a mandatory evacuation, yet still had no damage! The one on CT kept his power as the other son in Cambridge did too. It turned out that only our farm in RI lost power out of all of us. This meant that my friend Karin and her service dog Lucky were stuck taking care of our farm with no water, power or heat. This was stressful for us to learn about for Karin is also disabled and was not in good physical condition to be carrying water to the animals. Fortunately, the power outage only last a few days, but they were very difficult days for her to cope with. Who would ever have thought that leaving in the month of October would mean leaving when a hurricane would arrive!

So, back to the pain relief issue. My medication was dwindling as I waited for the package to arrive. The entire hospital staff was on alert for the box to arrive. Meanwhile, I had to play games with what was left of the medication and not take it as needed hourly, to be able to stay on top of my pain. It was very unnerving to wake up in the morning and see on the chart in my room as to how much medicine was left. As the storm continued and my medicine got lost in transit, I was running out of options and not getting the pain relief needed. A guardian angel suddenly resolved my troubles, a pharmacist named Joe. He had heard my plight and took me on and searched until he found a compound pharmacy that would help make some medication for me until my order arrived. In the meantime, he over rode his state law and allowed me to return back to Picc line medication of toradol, normally only allowed for five days due to high risk of kidney damage. They decided to monitor my blood daily and I knew as soon as the results came in showing changes, that this medication would have to be stopped. Fortunately, the timing worked out perfect, for the medication they made for me arrived the day I had to stop the medication. He knew I had no options left after major surgery with bone involvement. We somehow made it through the issues of delayed medication in time, but we were pretty rattled to watching the results of the hurricane damage. It took months to hear from all I knew it its path for I had grown up in NJ and many of my friends were in harms way of Sandy.

When it appeared that things were calming down for us, Stu decided one day to drive to a coffee shop and get us a treat. He left using a car that Peter and Beth Stillmank let us borrow. They had taken us into their home for years and put us up along with letting Stu use their car. When we had discovered that there was housing for out of state people near the hospital a few years after meeting them, we decided to stop imposing on them at their home but did still borrow their car for the two weeks. So, Stu went off and it suddenly felt fun that we were going to have a treat and life was going to calm down. Well, that assumption was wrong. Within a few minutes, Stu walked back into the room with a troubled look on his face. It seem that the car had a piece in the front that was suddenly dangling down and using the car was not going to be an option. The car had to be towed and repaired but we had a problem! Stu had only thirty dollars in his pocket having left all the money and credit card forty minutes away where he was staying. And, we discovered that few in the hospital lived in the immediate area and being out in the country, no one knew where to look for help! I thought Stu was going to break down and cry. Here we were in WI, with someone else's car, not knowing where to turn to or how we were going to pay for the repair. And then, another guardian angel walks in. The security man, Aaron, arrived in the room having heard about our situation. This amazing person actually got the car towed and used his credit card to pay for the repair and trusted that we would pay him back. We don't know what we would have done without his help!

The stay in the second hospital was an amazing as the other one. People were kind and supportive. I love having my surgeries in WI for the people have literally adopted us in as family. It was sad to have to say goodbye but to be going home was a wonderful feeling. The trip home started off amazing for we were actually placed in first class on the first flight. I was able to get comfortable and literally slept through the entire flight. However, luck ran out when it was time for the second flight. We ended up boarding the smallest flight where I was never able to properly able to put the leg out. I had to bend and twist to try to fit in place with my immobilizer on. Thank goodness I am a small person!

Well, it seems that arriving home should have ended this craziness, but one more thing happen to our shock. When we arrived to our home state of RI, we worked our way down to baggage where I was to report in, return the borrowed wheelchair and then switch to the one waiting for me to borrow until the new one was sent to our home. Well guess what? The people were expecting us and we're so excited to have me transition to the chair waiting, but there was a big problem. I was arriving immobilized and non-weight bearing, but the chair the had waiting for us was not correct. The legs we were given to attach with the chair were only to be used in a ninety-degree angle, knees bent. Now tell me, how was I supposed to bend my knees with an immobilizer on? So, that was when my emotions had had it and proceeded to cry in front of these very kind people. I was tired, in pain from the last flight and now just plain frustrated with the situation. We ended up having to take the WI wheelchair home and eventually make arrangements to return it to them when the replacement was brought out to the house a few days later.

This was a journey we would rather not remember too much!! The only reason this experience was not blocked out already is that it was the most recent experience we had when writing this chapter!

Melting Slowly

It suddenly occurred to me one day that life resembles a candle. You are born into this new body. The new baby tissue is so soft and the future is bright as life awaits you! And then in time, your body begins the process of aging, weakening and breaking the original "us" down. We can try hard to try to slow or even stop this process, but in time, the body and aging wins, not us!

So think about it, the candle is similar. It starts out firm, complete, attractive and appealing to the eye. In time, the candle is lit and the slow melting away begins. The candle is really never as beautiful as when it is first set out. Once first lit, the changes are apparent. In time, you almost wonder if it is worth keeping the poor thing since the sides are covered with the dripped, melted wax and looks like a useless stump. Some of us just discard that last stub while others have trouble letting it go. As with the body, we can't stop that process of the melting of the candle.

So what do we learn from this? We can't stay young, we can't stay that perfect little baby, life moves forward whether we want to accept this or not. We need to look again at that candle stub and remember that although it is not longer that beautiful new one, it does still hold light, still can spread warmth and can still have a purpose, despite its aging. And for us, the same exists. We will age, but we still need to remember that we can still have value in life. We may not look young and healthy, but we still breath, have passion and should still have purpose. So, are you going to throw that candle stub out, are you going to give up on us that are no longer considered youthful and healthy? Let's hope not. All things in life are slowly melting but to cope with this natural process, we need to remember the gifts we have been given.

Waves

I realize that my life might as well be out in the ocean for I seem to be riding waves all the time. Sometimes, I am so lucky and the wave takes me down into a wonderful moment, and yes, I meant to use the word moment. The good days are far and few between as Ehlers-Danlos progresses in my body.

Another example of riding the waves living with EDS happened just yesterday. I received an unexpected call to book me for a follow up CT scan on my chest. I asked them who was ordering this and assumed it was a mistake for no one had ever mentioned that this was needed. Of course, this call came in late on a Friday, so I spent the entire weekend pushing this out of my mind and assuming I was going to cancel this appointment when I was able to connect with my pulmonologist. He had traveled out of the country back in January, and his co-workers had ordered the CT to check out my floppy trachea. Two doctors had called me back individually from his office, each telling me what I am unfortunately use to hearing, that they didn't see anything strange. But what they never told me, was the rest of the report. So, when I connected with my doctor, I was shocked to hear that the repeat test WAS necessary since they did find new nodules in the left lung. So, another wave to ride – will this turn out to be the progression of my sarcoidosis in the lungs, which is not good news, or something that will have to be biopsied, clearly not good news or could this just be a misreading of the test. So, we wait on hold for the test and results. The bottom line is, if I ever test positive for cancer, treatment will not be an option with this body. I would not be able to cope with the reactions to radiation or chemotherapy! So, a diagnosis would be a fatal diagnosis for me. So, we ride this wave with fingers crossed!

The results did come in the next day and this time, I lucked out. The nodules are shrinking. And.....so comes the shrinking of concern and compassion that I experienced in that brief moment that they thought this might be malignant. Back to the life of people not already recognizing that my life is on the line every day, painful, unpredictable and slowly taking me away, piece by piece.

Too many times, I am riding that wave that tries to take me under. I seem to hit pockets of time that can take me backwards with more pain than ever. The moment comes out of nowhere, but I usually know when I wake up, that this is going to be a day of struggle. Unfortunately, that day turns into days and even weeks in a row. It is nuts but at one point of my life, way before becoming burdened with the horrors of living with EDS, I dreamed how much fun it would be to look into that crystal ball and see the future. Today, there is no way I want to know what is coming next. All I can do is hold on tight and try to ride these waves that keep coming at me. I wonder if I will be able to ride the wave to shore and walk away from all this?? I know, dream on

Why Bother?

This is almost embarrassing to share, but I am guessing someone reading this will be able to relate to this. I have had times when the news is just so overwhelming, that I have actually quietly in my mind said to myself "then why bother?". As the news on my condition kept getting more negative a few years back when I wasn't able to gain weight for three years, my breathing episodes were increasing and the picture wasn't too positive, I one day decided to stop dental flossing. That sounds like no big deal, but what I realize looking back was I was giving up. To floss was one more thing to do which is not my favorite, so being stuck in this deteriorating body, why not just stop doing it? But in time, things did improve through the use of the Vecttor treatment and life seemed to be back at my doorstep for me to try to embrace more. I have learned to not as quickly take on that attitude. Time can change a lot, not always as we want, but there is a chance for improvement. The human mind is pretty amazing. We need to fight that instinct of believing all is lost and try to hold on with hope.

What Defines Me?

We tend to define ourselves by what we do in life. For a long time, I was defined as the mother of four, the master swimmer, high school coach and an eighth grade social studies teacher. So, what does that make me today? Am I supposed to be defined as the disabled person? This is just not the label I want to live with! So, I have worked hard to still live a productive life despite living with these disabilities. I see myself as the person advocating for others instead. With my husband, we spend energy advocating for marriage equality, medical marijuana, and people living in pain and with arthritis, among other things. These topics feel positive and make me realize that I don't have to be remembered as that poor girl that got a raw deal. Instead, I hope to be remembered as the person that took on the challenge and made something with life despite the numerous challenges being presented daily. I choose to be defined by my actions, not my conditions!

Finding Purpose   10/29/07

Gone
Children now adults
Moved away
Exciting careers
Lives with passion
Exciting to watch unfolding

Career
Gone due to my disability
Left are those priceless moments
A wonderful time

Mobility wavering
Legs and feet unstable
On and off with a cane
Or the wheelchair

Surgeries
Up to fourteen now
Still two more planned on the horizon

So, what is my purpose?
Acceptance of my circumstance
Facing the truth while not giving in
Trying to stay safe
Trying to stay healthy
Loving my husband, which I don't have to even try to do!

It Hurts Like Hell

Trying to remain as positive as possible
Trying to control the pain
Trying to stay educated
Trying to help others

This is my life
I must live it without asking why me?
I must see and value my purpose

How Can We Laugh?

I am sure there are people that hear about what we are facing with my medical issues that wonder – how can they be laughing? Well, laughter is amazing medicine and should be included in your daily life. Just today, Stu and I went to the skin doctor for our six-month check. I ended up with two unexpected biopsies and Stu was sent off to the pharmacy to buy medicine to put on his face to kill off pre cancerous cells. This medicine will cause his skin to become very red and blotchy for a few weeks! We literally laughed as we compared notes of our appointments. Guess it may sound sick that we found this funny, but that has been our reaction for some time as more and more negative health news comes into our lives. Laughter is cleansing, to say the least. Give it a try! There is so much that happens to our lives that is just plain out of our control, so somehow just laughing at the insanity that more is coming your way actually helps to put it in perspective.

Happiness Is An Attitude —

"We either make ourselves miserable, or happy and strong.
The amount of work is the same"
(This was a quote my sister sent to me years ago that I hung in the
entrance to my classroom door. I love living by this motto!)

Laugh With Me   1 / 28 / 07

Inside of me is a balloon that is filled
Do you wonder what I have filled it with?
There is passion for life
There is compassion towards others
There is love that is beyond words,
Love towards my husband, my children, family and friends
There is so much in this balloon that I have enough to cope,
So, please learn to laugh with me

As I walk with my leg braces
trying not to catch the inside bars between my knees to prevent falls,
Laugh with me
At least I have these braces to help me still experience the privilege of
walking

As I try to adjust to my collar that goes from waist up,
Laugh with me
At least I have one last option to try to prevent more instability
of the neck
The last resort is surgery
I would rather not have to learn to walk again and have the neck
Fused
So, laugh with me as I learn to tolerate this

As I announce my next surgical stabilization
Laugh with me
At least it gives me hope for better quality of life

And someday,
Laugh with me when I look into your eyes
knowing you well
But I forget your name
Laugh with me, please
Know it's the disease, not the love I have towards you.

So, laugh with me as I progress
My life is good
For I have that filled balloon,
It helps me cope

I've Crossed The Line 4/1/07

The time has come,
I have now crossed the line

I was that person that swam,
walked,
tried snow and water skiing,
Camping, bowling,
I was that person that made plans and traveled
I was healthy, took no medications
I was strong
I was full of life

But today, I've crossed that line
Today, I have transitioned over as a disabled person
I no longer can swim,
Nor walk any distance
Bowling? I can't lift more than five pounds
I consider myself still healthy
But I must depend of medications to keep some organs functioning
No, I don't consider myself strong any more
I am alive, however and still full of wonder,
But I have crossed that line

The changes are huge
The loses are hard to count
Life is not what I expected
But I breathe,

ELLEN LENOX SMITH

I am here,
and I will continue to discover my new life with this transition
The challenge is huge
I have crossed over because I am ready

Wait For Me 4/3/08

Hey, I use to make it to first, second or third place
I was a swimmer
Look at me now
Could you please wait for me?

I don't have the same speed
I don't have the same endurance
Clarity is muddled

With progression of Ehlers Danlos
I am lucky to even get into the water
Numerous surgeries
Recuperations
Casts, splints and immobilizers
Slipping vertebrate

Many days are being stolen from me
But, I refuse to give up or give in
Stabilize, exercise, and follow instructions
That's my life
So, wait for me
*I am slower, but **I AM still here***

Rising To The Surface   3/8/08

Life with Ehlers-Danlos Syndrome
I use to describe that I had to tread water
To stay above the pain
To stay on top of the losses
To keep my emotions in check

But, with its progression, that job is changing
I now realize I tread less
I now wake up to a new assignment
I must rise to the surface each morning
After accomplishing that,
Then I can then return to my familiar treading

I must rise up to get to the top
To breath
To value life
To appreciate the good in my life
To meet that challenges presented to me

Treading
Rising to the top
What will be the next assignment to cope?

It Just Is

There are so many questions
So few answers
Things happen
Things can't be taken back
A split moment can change so much

Why an incurable disease?
Why is it progressing so rapidly?
Why did people question the truth?
Why must I live life like this now?

The answer?
It just is….
We can't control all
We can't find blame for most
We can't spend life feeling bitter

What we do have is the capability to cope
We can see the challenges in a positive light
We can continue to have awe as the sun rises and sets
As the seed blooms into a plant
As the next generation is born to carry on
We have that control
So, it just is that things happen,
But how we deal with the events is our responsibility
Waiting…

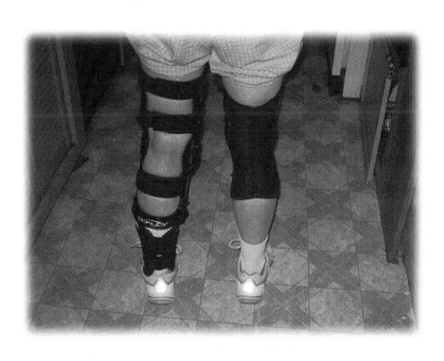

Two Steps Ahead, One Behind

We don't like to admit it, but we do talk with ourselves throughout our days and especially as we try to work out issues that arrive in life. I have to do a lot of talking with me when I slip backwards. I so desperately want to be back to myself, pain free, and mobile. However, I no sooner seem to make progress and then slip back again. And when this happens, I have to talk with myself and put these emotions of almost panic, disappointment and defeat in perspective.

Let me give you an example of taking two steps forward and then one backwards. I recently began the journey of transitioning from wearing a leg brace five months later from my twenty-first surgery. The goal has always been to be weight bearing. I have found that the times I have had to live in a wheelchair has done serious damage to this body. So, I have made a conscious decision to try to get back on these legs and endure too many surgeries and long recuperations. When I was assigned at physical therapy to walk without the brace for ten minutes, I suddenly started to notice a strange sensation in the left, good side. We stopped my walking, checked all out and found me still holding my position. However, when I woke up the next morning, pain had developed not only in the foot, but also in the tibia. I just couldn't believe that this could be happening to my good, presently non-surgical leg. It took a full week of having to correct the subluxations, along with lots of icing, to get this to settle down and hold again. Here I was five months post-op having to face issues with the other leg and foot that had already been surgically corrected. This issue happens constantly. I no sooner try to correct a problem to only seem to come apart at another seam!

Another example of two steps ahead, one behind just happen today. I was finally feeling like these past horrific three weeks of pain from constantly having double up-slips, along with the spine slipping out like jelly was coming to an end. I seem to have episodes that can last for weeks and then just seem to settle down. I had just finished walking the driveway, successfully walking for seven minutes without the surgical leg or reconstructed feet shifting out. This was exciting to accomplish, I was happy and hopeful.

I finish this walk and then noticed our gorgeous feral cat under my handicap ramp waiting for his treat I bring each day to him. So, I went inside, grabbed his treat and came out to the ramp to give it to him. After setting the food down, I noticed one of our indoor cats was eating his treat, so I reached down and grabbed some to set closer to the feral cat, under the ramp. Like a total idiot, as I bent down, I put my weight onto the ramp railing, forgetting that it was actually broken. I had set it up in the correct position so visually it would look normal, a few days earlier. Well, the rest of the story was not a pretty picture. Down I went onto the ramp, right onto my surgical knee and onto my wrist. I could hear the damage happening in the fall. I got to PT to find that I had moved the patella, along with the tibia and fibula. After he corrected these, I still felt strange in the foot. I had also subluxed the foot and it took him a good chunk of the time from my cranial appointment to make these corrections. Hopefully in time, this will all settle down and be forgotten, but it is so hard to have put all these months into recuperation to have one split second of your life put those corrections in jeopardy.

So, life with Ehlers-Danlos means taking two steps ahead and one step backwards, over and over. As I said, I have to counsel myself emotionally to not panic and assume all has been lost. I talk and reason with myself all the time to get through these emotionally times of let down.

Throwing It Away   2/22/08

Can I believe in this?
Can I buy into the concept that improvement can be on the horizon?
I want to believe,
But luggage has to be dumped first

Needed to thrown away:
Being scared of my body
Wavering of believing there can be better
Questioning if the ending of pain would override the desire to live
Wondering if I have enough inner strength to keep fighting

It's all getting so old
False hopes
More pain
More surgeries
Less mobility
Tired
Struggling

Can I dig deeper?
Can I really find enough hope to do what is needed?
Can I throw enough away?
For if I don't, how can I improve?

My Legs   2/13/07

You have taken me many places
We have swum miles together
We have walked through the reservoir and up mountains
We have danced for hours
We have lain on the beaches
We have ridden on bikes

You have been good to me
You have given me so many opportunities to see and do things
I never really dwelled on thinking about you
I just expected you would always be a part of my life

But you, my legs, are growing loose and weak
You have done a good job and now it is time for you to rest
I will keep fighting to hold on to you
But I realize that time is getting short
I understand now that you were a gift to me that I just expected and ignored
Now as you are considering leaving me, I wish I could ask for a second chance.
I would appreciate you each day and care for you even better
Would you consider giving me that chance?

Education Alert

When you live with a rare condition, it is always a wise idea to get involved with spreading the awareness of your condition. I spend a lot of time, especially meeting new medical people, explaining what Ehlers-Danlos does to your life. I have tried to get involved with awareness through various events. Stu and I host a yearly event in our state to honor pain awareness in September. Through this event, we are able to address this and other conditions that cause pain, disability or just a change in lifestyle. I recently even met a woman at a meeting and found out her husband is the person at Brown University that books the medical students schedule and is himself also involved with researching through NIH grants. I asked her is she thought he would mind me contacting him to request to be connected with the person on staff that might consider having me come in and give a short presentation on Ehlers-Danlos. To my shock, she said that he is the right person and gave me his email. I wrote him that night and by the next day, had a beautiful email back from him suggesting this Fall would be the first he could set this up and he plans on calling. I am so excited to think that if just one of these medical students happens to remember what I expose them to about my condition, then that person properly diagnoses a patient with my condition, that means years cut off of the unknown that most of us have to face!

Other places I have turned to is NIH, where I discovered they were doing research on my condition. We have presented to the Blue Cross nurses in our state, the physical therapy programs at the University of RI and also in our neighboring state of CT, at UCONN, along with presenting twice now at the EDS national conference. My goal always is to help future generations inflicted with my condition to have an easier path to follow than most of us have had to experience. To get diagnosed in a timely manner, get proper pain control along with an understanding on how to safely live life with the condition, can really help someone's life to improve. So, get out there and make a difference – help educate others about your condition!

My Manager

For sometime, I have joked about my friend, Joanne, head of RIPAC, being "my manager". Joanne will occasionally contact me to connect me with a media requests. It has included newspaper, radio and TV interviews. At times, I wondered why she was selecting me. However, I finally seem to understand why me. I am presently sixty-five years old, been using medical marijuana in our state for eight years, a former teacher in the Burrillville Middle School, am educated, and able to represent the older population in our state. It is important, as we try to educate the public to this program, that they see representation that does not look like druggies. But, due to this exposure, I am now considered the "marijuana lady" in RI. I want to be remembered for making a change in people's knowledge about the advantages of using this medication for pain, but also want others to be aware of more about me! I am honored to be able to meet with the media and hope that we have helped to make a dent in people's understanding of the use of this as medication.

I love teaching people that when you use this medication for pain, you do not get high or stoned. You get pain relief, and that's it! Also, there are no overdoses from this, no organ damage and no reported deaths. So, therefore, we have to share the truth about this way to relieve pain!

Spinning

After I returned home from bilateral foot stabilization with two casts on the legs and totally non-weight bearing for five months, I had my first experience of dizziness that changed my life forever. I was set up in a hospital bed in the living room at this time and was getting ready to close my eyes for the night. Upon beginning to doze off, I suddenly felt like I was falling off a steep cliff and suddenly felt spinning like I had never experienced in my life. Stu recognized something was terribly wrong and brought a chair next to my bed and proceeded to spend a good chunk of the night sitting up next to me making sure I was okay. I had had one other time in my life getting dizzy after returning from a wonderful cruise that my sister took me on to celebrate my fiftieth birthday. In time, that horror drifted away, but this experience was much more severe and as I mentioned, was one more sign that things were deteriorating in this body. Ever since this, I have had episodes at night when I actually get blockage on my breathing. Thanks to service dog Maggie, I am protected at night. When the trachea bends and or the sternum slips down, she senses my problems and stimulates me to moving positions by licking me over and over. I appreciate her loyalty to me and sometimes have to not have a moment of concern as I watch her age like the rest of us. What happens to my life if I outlive her? Is it possibly for another dog matched to me someday to know what is happening and also save me? My solution to this is the following – either I leave this earth before her or she just remains the age of seven forever and never grows older.

Not Yet! 6/28/07

There you are knocking again
I have felt your presence before
You make my chest feel so strange
You make me feel something I'd rather not
You make me believe that it is my time to leave
And experience that last breath

But, I have a message to you
Not yet!
I have dreams to live
Weddings to attend
Grandchildren to meet and fall in love with
A best friend to enjoy the rest of life with

Someday, it will be time
I will know , for I will be ready
I will welcome you and allow you to start my final journey
But not yet!
I am meant to still continue on

If I Don't Wake Up 2/13/07

If I don't wake up
It will be okay
The sun will still shine
The rain will still fall
The seasons will keep changing
New designs and development will continue on

If I don't wake up
It will be okay
Life will continue on
The birds will still sing
The gardens will still bloom
Families will keep growing

If I don't wake up
It will be alright
I will leave you to continue to enjoy all the gifts of life
And you will enjoy them knowing that
I am now in peace, away from the daily pain
It will be all right.

Brain Fog

When I was speaking in DC, in 2013, a question was asked of our panel at the end as to how you can tell the difference from just temporary pain to chronic pain. I asked to respond, for I immediately remembered the horror of being in such pain while still teaching that I was unable to remember my student's names. I literally had to keep a seating chart in front of me to respond to them by name. The brain fog I can experience can be so overwhelming that I am not able to think, act and respond in a normal manner.

Brain fog is a real experience and is terribly discerning. The one thing I have found that can help relieve this when it happens is to get to my manual cranial therapist. He is able to unlock the shifting in my head that is happening, allowing the proper flow of spinal fluids. Please don't think you are nuts when this happens to you. Find some source of relief. You can try many different approaches such as acupuncture, yoga, and reiki. Just don't accept this, find a way to help alleviate this condition. I know how horrible it feels to not be able to act and think. You don't deserve this and need to be proactive and find some type of relief that works for you.

Fog Again

It's back again
The cloudy haze
The confusion
The feeling of unknown
The feeling of drifting away
Yes, the fog is back

It's happened many times
It always shakes me
It makes me feel so lost
It makes me feel so alone
It makes me question the point

Ehlers-Danlos Syndrome brings on my fog
When it drifts back in,
It makes life a daily struggle
It makes trying to stop the progression seem almost hopeless
It makes you dig so very deep to find meaning
It makes you question your symptoms

Well, I am trying today
Can I force the fog to thin?
Can I find a sunny opening?
Can I step away from it enveloping me?

It's my job to find the solution

It Hurts Like Hell

Fog is not wanted again
Needed instead is hope, dreams and less pain
I know that is out there, apart from the fog.

Moments When Life just Seems Out Of Control

It is amazing how one-day alone can seem to get out of control. I will share an example of what my day was like yesterday. It began waking up feeling just horrible. All I did was go to bed, putting my BI-PAP Advance breathing mask on, legs over a pillow to keep my back flat and settled into my hospital bed. I never dare roll over for it immediately causes the spin to shift out. So, off to sleep I went having had one of my better days, but this was clearly not going to be another good day.

Waking up feeling that lousy means an up slip. Well, it turned out to be an up slip on both sides, which causes the thinking process to almost want to shut down. But, despite how I ever wake up feeling, it is a day to live and sometimes figure out how to get through.

We went off to my heart appointment thinking this would just be a nice time to see a doctor that is so pleasant and kind, and we would just be catching up with life. But instead, he had to explain that the Echo showed markers indicating that I was developing stiffness in the heart that in time would lead to congestive heart failure. I am now assigned to weigh myself daily and if I ever have a bad day and also notice that my weight has increased abnormally, and then I am to call and be put on a diuretic. Not the end of the world, but more news that isn't needed! And, I was feeling horrible with my double up slip.

Off we then went to my physical therapy and I called my dermatologist for the results on two biopsies he had to do the week before. Fortunately, the news was pretty good. One spot was safe and the other needs more freezing in a month – I can handle those results!

After my physical therapy appointment, where he had to fix the back, I then got into the call to a call that came in with results of the x-ray done on my surgical leg, surgery #21. It seems that the bones, after five months and ten hours a day with a bone stimulator on it, still have not healed. So, I am assigned to continue using the bone stimulator. Meanwhile. He also is concerned about a spot where he had removed two protruding screws that now have a hard spot in the area. He is ordering a CT scan to see if this could be caused by leakage from the ACL repair and the tibia drilling. Are we serious? Can there really be any more issues to have to accept and deal with?

So, we ended this day of extra pain and news we would rather have not had to face by going off to the Statehouse to testify. I was tired, concerned, yet felt I needed to still be that ambassador for the pain and arthritis foundations and stand up for others for their health care. I am glad we went for we learned a lot and were able to put aside the issues of the day!

Moments That Were Beyond Expectations

Stars Aligned

The Stars Are Aligned   11/01/06

Yes, the stars are aligned for me today
Have you ever heard of this happening?
There seems to be that magical day when everything falls into place
Today, is that day for me

When the stars are aligned for me,
I feel energetic
I feel the mind has more clarity
I feel that hopes and dreams can really be seen to fruition
I feel on top of the world

As I treasure this moment,
I know it won't last forever
So, I try to document, for safe keeping, the enlightened moments in
my mind

ELLEN LENOX SMITH

I allow myself to dream it will last forever
I must be grateful for whatever time is given to me to experience this
relief.

Today, I got to feel free
I could unburden my troubles and cast them to the wind
Today, the stars were aligned for me
I could be like you for a short moment.

I use to consider everyday pretty darn special, but living in pain, those days are more numbered. When first diagnosed, I was still teaching and was able to have an average of two good days a week when I felt in control and on top of my emotions and condition. But as time has progressed, those days are very infrequent.

When I am able to say I have a good day, it is now beyond my expectations. I can tell when I open my eyes, what type of day I am headed for. Waking to a good day, I don't have to feel jolted right away by pain. I am able to read the paper better, focusing with less dizziness. It is such an amazing treat and also a tease. I fall in love with the peace and clearness of the day and never want it to end.

For a number of years, I had read to my social studies classes the book called: Tuesday with Morrie. I loved the courage the man that was the focus of the book had knowing that he was slipping away with Lou Gehrig's disease. Never in my wildest dreams did I realize I was teaching not only them but also me, learning through his wise words how to cope with an incurable condition. I remember the author, a former student of this professor that was dying, asking him what he would do if he were given just one day to live life as he wished. I remember being shocked that all he wished for was a normal day – one that included reading the paper, having a good cup of coffee, taking a walk, swimming, and enjoying talking with a friend. Now that I am in a place like that, I totally get what he is saying. When I wake up to a day that the brain fog is dissipated, the thinking is working and action can be done, I am in my glory. I don't need to travel to Hawaii, spend a lot of money, or conquer the world. An amazing day for me is simple and calm – what I consider to be beyond my expectations.

I want to share an example of one of those special days that just seems to happen to you. My friend, Pam, picked me up to take me out on an adventure in the town to get a cup of tea and sit and talk. We arrived to the Village Bean to realize that there were three steps to get inside and at this point, six months past my last leg surgery, I still can't accomplish going up stairs without both the fibula and foot subluxing. So, since it was a gorgeous, warm spring day, we decided to sit outside. Before we knew it, Pam's husband Gerry drove by, parked and joined us. No sooner, when he was ready to leave, a former neighbor saw us sitting out there as she drove by, parked and joined us too. We were able to catch up on life, our children and our dreams. While sitting there listening, I suddenly noticed a dress hanging in the doorway at the store next door. Gerry went over for me and checked out the size and got the price. It was a beautiful second hand silk dress waiting for me to take it home! I literally put in on over my outfit to see if it might fit since I wasn't able to get into the dressing room inside. It was a perfect match! I will be able to use it for my niece's' wedding in Georgia in June.

So, there you have it – a moment not expected that turned out just magical for me. This day was certainly way beyond my expectations. I can't wait to have more of these days in the future!

My Perfect Day

So here is my perfect day. First, I would enjoy waking up feeling better than usual, enjoy the coffee, I would actually be able to read the paper without my aspen neck collar on! So, instead of scanning the paper due to dizziness, I would read the entire articles! I would then cook a breakfast that tasted good and wasn't restricted from dairy, soy, nightshade vegetable, and gluten. From there, we would go off to the pool and swim laps like I use to do when I was a master swimmer. I would not have to go to PT since everything would remain in position. I would actually be the one to drive us for the first time in about five years and we would come home and work in the garden. I would turn over the soil and begin to plant our organic garden, like I use to be able to do for years. I would soak in those sunrays onto my face and enjoy the fact that I could walk on uneven ground, which is not an option now with both feet fused to hold them together. After working outside, I would then have a tasty lunch followed by a pleasant rest time where I would cuddle with service dog Maggie along with a few of our cats.

In the afternoon, I would sit on a chair outside, listening to the birds singing and READ. What a treat that would be! My neck would not hurt and the sun would tan my face and make me look healthy and alive. After that break, we would go for a walk in the neighborhood with my own my legs instead of my scooter. That would be a treat for I use to walk at least three miles at a time with the dogs and miss it. Stu and I would then go off to get a treat along with a special cup of coffee.

Preparing dinner would be fun for I would be able to cut the food myself instead of having to ask Stu since the pressure causes the arms and chest to sublux. We would enjoy the meal watching the news and then retreat to our studies after. I would email good friends and have a conversation with Diane, my friend since first grade. She would want to talk with me because I like this, I would be representing health, instead of sadness, which turns so many away without meaning to. Around nine, we would gather in the living room and watch one of our favorite shows before retiring to our bedroom.

That's it - simple pleasures – simple requests – just being able to return to the life I knew and always loved to live. Maybe this will be my day tomorrow? Or, maybe this will just have to remain in my memories. Either way, it is my idea of being perfect!

Lost And Found   10/20/06

Lost

Clarity of mind
Normal use of the body
Swimming laps in the lake
Sleeping in any position I want
Digging in the garden
Long walks through the woods
Satisfaction of yard work and housework
Eating whatever I want
Touching

Found

Acceptance instead of blame
Unbelievable inner strength man is given to tap
Friendship filled with compassion and sincerity
Justification to ask and receive help
A growing family circle
A deeper relationship than ever imagined
A family bond that is priceless
The beauty and gift of life

My rules have changed
I've lost
But more importantly, I've found
Have you checked out the lost and found lately?

If I Could Wish

Imagine having the opportunity to actually make a list of wishes and have them come true! I would first wish for all the friends that meant the world to me decide to reach out to me and include me back in their lives. I would also wish that my extended family understood what we were facing daily and reach out to me more frequently and actually ask how I was doing, or how my husband was doing. I know they love me, but everyone gets so caught up in their lives that I am not sure they have ever begun to understand what this condition has done to our daily lives.

And adding to that with family, I would wish for them to understand that I am not making this up and face nights wondering if I will wake up again. I would have to add having the body that was able to hold my grandchildren and be able to get down to their level to play would be amazing. It is tough to have to accept that, Papa Stu, is their hero while I have to melt to the side with a smile on my face and not keep up like he can. I would also add to those wishes being able to swim again, drive again, walk on my yard that is uneven ground, and speaking of walking – be able to walk many miles like I use to do. Ehlers-Danlos is a silent, lonely struggle. So, we struggle alone without both our siblings, at times.

So, I guess it is summed up by the following – not having my condition be invisible to others so people comprehend how hard Stu and I are trying to make the best of a horrific condition that is slowly taking me down. Are you able to grant me these wishes?

138

Caregiver

I don't think people really take a lot time to consider the time and commitment a caregiver makes to help another person. My husband, Stu, has totally dedicated his life to helping me get through but I know this isn't coming for free. The stress he has to cope with as each new diagnosis comes to us or just living daily knowing that I now have a few things wrong with the body that can take me out at any time is just overwhelming. For a long time, it was just the breathing issues we had to face when the Bi-Pap Advance can't do it's job due to when the trachea gets twisted and/or the sternum slips inwards. But we have now added new news that the heart is beginning to harden and will eventually cause congestive heart failure. These concerns at time seem surrealistic. It really doesn't seem possible that in my mid sixties that we are facing this.

Despite this tough news, Stu is always there for me. We mourn the losses that keep coming our way together and somehow, through drawing off each other's strength, find a way to return to laughing at life and being productive in any way possible. The many times we run to the state house to testify, may look to others as we are doing too much, but we do find the more we can reach out to help others and focus on things constructive beyond our medical issues is so helpful.

Do me a favor and be sure to think not just about the person that is not well, but also the person that is caring for them. Ask them how they are doing and if you can do anything to help them have a break. They are amazing people that have made a commitment to help one they love. This is not something you ever will dream will happen to your life and they need to be commended for doing the right thing. I have been one of those lucky ones that was blessed to be married to a man that didn't give up on me. But remember, someone that is a caregiver is living through this horror too and needs support.

Lifeguard Needed   11/15/06

I have just posted the opening
There is a full time position open for a life guard
Are you interested?

The requirements are:
Be able to keep a close watch at all times
Be strong when I am weak
Be able to keep me from danger
Be able to keep life safe through your guarding

All applicants will be considered
The most qualified will be chosen
You will be the one to protect me
You will be my "Life Guard"

Stuart Burns Smith   11/27/06
You Are the Reason for US

Stuart Burns Smith
Husband
Father
Best Friend
The love of my life
You are the reason for us

You asked me to write you a poem
My reaction was to shut down
Why?
It took me awhile to understand why no words would spill out
The reason was,
I couldn't imagine how I'd put into words something that would be so
painful if it is was to be someday taken away from me
So, my words shut down.
But, I knew, you are the reason for us

But, now I know the truth of that reaction
The truth is,
You are the soul of my life
You are the reason I don't give up and rise to each new day
You are the person that always takes time to listen and understand
You are the one that never gives up on me
You are the one that comforts and supports me and makes me laugh
You are committed to me

You are living those words from our vows" in sickness and in health"
daily
You are what love is about
You are the reason for us

Our lives are so beautifully interconnected
Our interests have continued to bloom through the years
Our children are the biggest gift we could have ever been given
Our relationship remains solid and priceless
You will always be my best friend, my soul mate, the reason to live on
You are the reason for us, and I thank you for that.

Merry Christmas,
Love,
Ellen

Why Are You Hyper Today?

One day, which happen to be what I describe as my "gift day", I was driving to PT for my legs. I noticed that my husband had pulled my PT into his office to tell him something. Being a nudge, I wasn't going to be satisfied until I found out what this big discussion was about. It turned out that my husband had joked with him to watch out, that since today was a good day, I became overly excited and talkative. I laughed with them when I heard this and joined in on the comment. But to be honest with you, that night, as I was trying to sleep with my sternum slipped in and the trachea bent, thus making breathing hard despite a Bi-Pap St machine on, I thought back on that joking comment and actually felt the tears roll down my cheek. What was happening to my life? Was I turning into this hyper person on my good moments?

I have to agree that I can feel myself just on top of the world when I have a break from pain. Suddenly, food is fun to eat and taste, dreams seem possible again, and just being able to breath with no discomfort is such a treat. But have I become a hyper acting person during this moment? Do I now have to also counsel myself into how to behave during my good days too? Truly, this body goes into talking sessions reminding myself to smile, stay positive, believe there can be better when I am at my worst with pain. I have always stayed very conscience with how I come across on the bad days, that I assumed being free and excited would be expected and embraced by others on a good day. But, I guess I now have to monitor myself on those few positive days I get. Where is the spontaneity in my life?

Hope – Needed To Hold On To Life

I would like to share an example how holding on to hope can make the most horrible situation seem promising. We went to the Chiari Institute in Great Neck, NY for my recheck form tethered cord surgery in 2007. During the discussion, we had to address the other issues I was facing. The most concerning was hearing that my neck did need to be fused, but due to my severe osteoporosis, surgery would not be an option since it would most likely cause the plates and screws to pull out, due to the weak bones. Without having expected to hear this news, I confronted the doctor with the question I needed the answer to when Stu walked out of the room to use the restroom. I needed to know what I was to expect knowing that we could not surgically correct this issue. The answer I had to listen to be beyond my imagination for I was told that I would eventually become bedridden and choke on my mucus for my final days. I looked at him, shared that I didn't expect this to be me, but if it was the case, would I be able to sign a consent form and have him try the surgery anyway in attempts to save my life. I said this and then wondered what I had just done. How was this doctor going to respond to such a request? But, he looked me right in the eyes and shared that he

146

knew what I was asking of him and that I had his word that he would do that for me.

So, here is an example of how holding on to hope gives you a chance for life. I was given a pretty grave diagnosis that we don't share with many, yet, we drove from NYC to RI feeling happy because we did not feel abandoned by this doctor. Instead, he was willing to put his career statistics potentially on the line in hopes of trying to save my life. Stu and I were realistic in knowing that this surgery would be dangerous and most likely not successful, but for me to know I could turn to him if things did get that bad is so comforting and kept me feeling hopeful!

This doctor kept me on his radar since 2007. Two years ago, he started to communicate that he had found a shorter screw procedure that he believed would hold for me and I had a short window of time to address this. So, October 28, 2015, we drove to NY to have the C-1, C-2 fusion that took nine hours living now with high hopes of a longer and more productive future.

I still get shocked by telling this story and how the doctor's comments made me feel. Encouragement and support go such a long way in coping with the unknown.

Digging 4/28/08

There are times life is like digging a hole
I wish I meant a hole that shows progress
But, I am referring to one that isn't making gains,
It's like trying to dig in the sand
The deeper I go,
The water seeps in
The sides keep collapsing

Each time I think I am working to move forward,
The sides seem to cave in with more to cope with
As I am recovering from one surgery,
The reality of the next one is already known

I would love to stop digging
I would love to walk in my garden
Stroll on the beach
Walk in the woods
But, this is not happening
Progression of Ehlers-Danlos is the reason
I have to keep digging
Digging against the forces
And, hope that I can still somehow overcome this syndrome

Hope

You have Ehlers-Danlos Syndrome
Presently, there is no cure
You will most likely progress
You will most likely sublux
  Feel increased pain
  Experience many losses
Your life will change course

However,
Keep smiling despite it all
Keep dreaming
Keep searching for answers
Keep being as positive as you can
For, it doesn't take much to find hope

A simple hug
A moment of compassion
A listening ear
A new set of eyes
A new EDS friend
An old friend that finally understands
We can get through this with hope on our side

Miracles Can Happen – My Legs Are Back

Six years ago, I started to be able to go into a large store with my legs. Instead, Stu has had to push me in my wheelchair. It just has been the life I have had to try to accept. However, I know that with bones coping with severe osteoporosis, the worse thing I can do is be non weight bearing. So, I made the conscience decision to keep plugging along, surgery after surgery, to attempt to get the fibula, patella and tibia to hold in place. A few years back, after spending months in the wheelchair, I was shocked that I was told I the hospital that I was walking wrong. I literally had to learn HOW to walk again. They kept telling me the steps were too short and my foot wasn't rolling properly. I just couldn't believe that I had to think ahead to figure out how to walk correctly again. We just take all this for granted. To this day, I have to remind myself to roll the left for since after two foot surgeries and some nerve damage, I frequently forget the correct process you all just do!

After twenty-three surgeries, primarily on my legs, I had actually made the progress I had dreamed about. I have to admit there were many moments of doubt and wondering why I was being so stubborn to put myself through all this. It has been a tough battle to get through due so many heartbreaking setbacks. I have been in physical therapy for these legs for years now, done all that has been asked of me, and after each surgery, dreamed that someday the legs would finally hold and I would be able to walk into a store on my own.

Well, I learned that dreams can come true for that dream came to fruition! I was allowed to try walking into our favorite store, Whole Foods. I actually walked up and down the aisle with my legs cooperating, totally pain free and holding in place. I have never been more excited than to have this first moment. I wish I had never had any doubts, but I am human and having to face your bones slips even after surgery to correct the issue is pretty hard to swallow.

For the past two years, however, I started to lose that ability. It seems that walking long distances or on any uneven ground again started to bring back some problems with the feet and legs subluxing again. But, as I heal from the neck fusion, I have high hopes that in time, I will be able to regain what I had accomplished. So for now, I am back to having to use the scooter or wheelchair in a large store.

I will never take this gift for granted, even if it didn't last forever. I am lucky, have worked hard, and will not allow myself to ever totally give up with the hope to walk again. I today, can't always achieve that walk through a large store, but being able to walk into appointments, walk around the house and in and out of the car are a huge gift when you have spent four years in a wheelchair.

Roads

I believe that there are still roads for us to follow, even when we feel that we have lost so much of life as we knew it. I have found that the roads I have now followed are as important than any I have ever been on. My disabilities have led me into new friendships and new meaning to my life and life in general. I never would have become an ambassador, advocate and been so willing to drop everything to help others. I do believe I have become a stronger person with much more meaning to my life due to having to cope with these conditions. I actually like myself more than ever and truly consider myself a happy person.

Below is a song whose words never leave my head that I want to share with you:

Roads   Sung by Chris Mann

"In this life that we are traveled, there are scars and there are battles where we roam. When we are lost or wherever we may go, they will always lead you home.

There are roads, that have led me to another, to a friend or to a lover I have known. For every turn, is a year that I have grown, as I walked along these roads.

Some are long and weathered; some will lead you through a storm. When you've gone astray, you will find your way, as you walk along these roads.

There were times, when I stumbled and I wondered, but every choice and every step, I don't regret. Cause I have lived, and I have loved like no other, I won't fear what lies ahead.

Some are long and some are weathered, some will lead you through a storm, when you've gone astray, you will find your way, as you walk along these roads.

They will one day lead me home…………."

Conclusion

Remember that we all have to face death and difficult issues in life. If you are like me with an incurable condition, then you have to face the possibility that your life will be shorter than others. However, someone else, who doesn't have that diagnosis, may walk outside tomorrow and be hit by a car and be instantly gone. Life does not always make sense and seem fair. So what do we learn from all this?

Try to not compare your problems with other people's issues. This is not a contest to see who has it worse. Instead, try practicing just caring about what others are facing too. Try to put yourself into their shoes. For those of you that are presently healthy, don't stop sharing your life with others that are living in pain. Believe me, it feels so sad when you find out someone you care very much about doesn't share with you because they feel is it unfair to you. People have the tendency to think that what they are going through could never come close in severity to what you are facing. That assumption actually makes it tougher to try to live life with pain. One wants to feel part of others lives. Let us tell you if we can't handle hearing about your trials, but I think you will find most of us want to feel still included in life – yours and ours! So, keep us in the loop, know it is healthy for us to refocus away from our problems and be reminded that we all have to face life's challenges.

Healthy or not, it is never too late to take time to get on board with how to improve the quality of your life. Despite the horrors of a tough diagnosis, you still have your life to live and how you do this is in your hands. Do you want to be that person that turns others off due to constantly complaining and talking about your hardship or do you want to be remembered as the person that took their condition on as a challenge? You will be shocked as to how much is still out there to do in life despite living with pain and/or an incurable condition. Try to think and live positive.

And notice all the amazing people and events that have come into your life due to what you are facing. Although many people that meant the world to you have faded, there are others that never would have entered your life if you were not facing what you are facing. I have found the unexpected friendships have been so rewarding. I love to listen to the song from the musical WICKED, called, For Good. It states: **"people come into our lives for a reason bringing something we must learn. Because I knew you, I have been changed for good!"** I thank all of you that have come into my life and helped me to become a better person. I may have two incurable conditions to cope with, but I like who I am today better than ever. My goal is to continue to reach out to help others and make their journey in life a little kinder.

Do These Symptoms Sound Like You?

We are born into our bodies and that is our norm, thus it is shocking when you realize your body is not acting the way it was meant to be. For many years, life seemed pretty normal. But, looking back, I was mentioning things to others and now realize they were very strange – like in high school having my palms of my hands turn black and blue after clapping at a dance and also asking which way to put my elbows while on the parallel bars in gymnastics. But, I lived my life as an active person, not realizing I was born with a rare condition called Ehlers-Danlos Syndrome, which was causing my collagen to be deformed. Thus, my ligaments and tendons are like overstretched elastic bands. This in turn allows joints to get too loose and causes painful subluxations, meaning partial dislocations.

Many others with this condition are like me and don't get diagnosed properly due to its rareness. It took me fifty-four years before a doctor recognized the symptoms and suggested what she thought was the problem. I had been sent to her due to a repeat bladder prolapse just two years after having the surgery to correct the sudden problem. She sent me off to a geneticist to confirm her suspicion before she would operate on me. I was grateful that she finally helped to put the pieces of the puzzle together for me. However, I was shocked to learn that at this time, it is an incurable condition.

So, what is one's life with EDS like? You have to spend your life being cautious with your every move. For instance, due to our laxity, a simple hug can cause the ribs and spine to move and sub lux. The incidents of the body shifting increases with age, as the pain does. Three things are very important to get evaluated with this condition. First of all, we are prone to having a tethered cord, meaning the cord could still be pulling down on the spine. If not corrected, this will potentially cause permanent kidney damage. The next thing to check for is instability of the neck. We need to wear neck collars in the car to be safe due to this and some will require stabilization of the neck to regain strength. The other thing you need to check for is Chiari I malformation, where the brain tissue protrudes into your spinal canal. This can be surgically corrected and would alleviate the headaches one has to endure with this condition. Also, many of us also deal with severe osteoporosis.

It is important to learn how to properly care for yourself with this condition. For instance, you should not lift more that five pounds or it would cause more pain in the body, straining the ligaments and tendons. The core needs to be strengthened since the muscles are responsible for not only their job, but are also on overload taking over the job of the ligaments and tendons. Many with this condition also tend to have issues with digestion, with numerous food reactions and issues with metabolizing drugs. Celiac disease is not uncommon for many of us to face. A manual therapist is a wonderful person to turn to for help for they can safely get you subluxations corrected. Also, if things persist, find a surgeon that understands the condition and is willing to use cadaver tendons to secure your joints.

Life with EDS is a constant challenge. Please help the next person you meet. Someday we dream of not only a cure but finding an understanding network of doctors to help us out. It is a lonely journey if you don't reach out to others.

You have any questions, feel free to contact me:

Ellen lenox smith

Ellen.smith2@gmail.com

401-474-0115

What Is EDS?   10/29/06

EDS

Every Day is a Surprise

Each Day you Slip

Energy is Depleted Seriously

Easily you Dislocate and Sublux

Equilibrium Desperately Slips

Episodes of Divorce and Separations are common

Energy is Depleted Seriously

Everyone Dreads needing Scooters

EDS

Efficient Diagnosis is Stressed

Effective Daily Strengthening is needed

Emphasize Digestive Supplements

*Employ Demeanor **Sheath** to protect from judgment*

Empty Dampened Spirits

EDS

Escape Dangerous Situations

Each Daughter and Son has a 50% chance of having it

Education is Desperately Suggested, so

Educate, Debate, Scholars needed

Enormous Dreams for Solutions are helpful

EDS

Ehlers-Danlos Syndrome

Everyone Dreads the Sacrifice

Each Desires Simplicity

EDS.....easy to describe, sad to live with

Who Invented This?   7/18/07

Congratulations!
Someone deserves the honor
Who is this person that invented this?

I am one of many who experiences your invention
We have pain
Rapid progression
Frequent subluxations
Numerous surgeries
Uncertainty
Frequent loses
We have your invention of EDS
So, congratulations
You may have gotten into us
But we are a stubborn bunch and we won't take this lightly
We will search on and someday,
we will be part of the solution to your mysterious invention
We will be part of the cure that will come!

You Too?   **4 / 29 / 07**

Meeting new people
Discovering connecting threads
New knowledge gained
New thoughts shared,
Not feeling alone
Sharing compassion towards one another
This is Happiness

But........
There is also sadness

Why?
Because you too have a chronic condition
You too have pain
You too have felt the unfair judgment
Searching and waiting for answers,
You too have losses

But we focus on happiness
We have good in our lives
We value a single moment that others would pass right by and ignore

We know what we want and are searching how to achieve it
We desire good health
Not the material tapestry others paint to live in
We want quality of life

ELLEN LENOX SMITH

To be recognized and respected for our courage
We don't give up
We live the life we have been given
And, we include a smile on our faces, despite our pain

So, welcome new friend
I am so happy to meet you
Yet sadden that you too must cope like me
But we will be there for each other

Articles Written for Pain News Network:

8 Tips for Patients Newly Diagnosed with **Ehlers-Danlos**

By Ellen Lenox Smith,
Columnist for Pain News Network

Ehlers-Danlos Syndrome (EDS) is a condition that causes one to be born with deformed connective tissue, the "glue" that holds the body together. At this time, there is still no cure to correct this problem, so living life with this condition means a accepting a certain level of chronic pain.

There are simple things to learn to live your life with EDS more safely. For instance, learning how to properly strengthen the muscles that are on overload doing their job, along with that of the useless ligament and tendons. Or understanding how certain twists and turns bring on other slippage of the body.

Living with Ehlers-Danlos Syndrome means, at times, a long, lonely and difficult journey burdened with a constant search for direction on how to try to create something resembling   a normal life. I am 65, but it wasn't until eleven years ago that I was finally given the correct diagnoses of something I was actually born with!

There have been times that I felt guilty for almost wishing I had been given a diagnosis of cancer -- for then the doors of hope, direction, plans and medical interest would have been with me at all times. Instead, as many other EDS patients have faced, we cope with the unknown, the judgment from friends and even family, the isolation, the confusion and the lack of consistent knowledgeable help.

All I ever wanted, when first diagnosed, was for someone to reach a hand out and guide me. That hand has never been there. So, instead, I have spent the past eleven years attempting to help prevent others from having to replicate my experience. I simply wish to assist other EDS patients avoid some of the uncertainty and stress that I was forced to experience. The task is often overwhelming and difficult, but you have no choice. This is the life you have been given to live.

With that in mind, I would like to make suggestions to the newly diagnosed, in hopes that your journey will begin safely by addressing these issues:

1. **Confirm with a knowledgeable geneticist that you have EDS.** If you get the feeling they do not understand or believe you have EDS, then go to another geneticist. I met with three before I was convinced and accepted the diagnosis.
2. **Mourn your losses.** It's okay and necessary to allow yourself to mourn the loss of your past life. Life will move on, but it will never be exactly as you have known it. As you go through

166

that process, remember you need to reach the goal of moving on.

3. **Address pain control.** You will need to accept that you can not take this journey on your own. You need to address your pain to have a chance of going back to living a normal life again. You might be like many of us and have trouble metabolizing certain medications. In that case, DNA drug sensitivity testing would help you to identify a compatible pain medication.

   Many respond beautifully to medical marijuana instead of opiates. It can be taken in a simple dose of oil at night, that not only allows you to sleep but also carries pain relief to the body even into the next day.

4. **Be evaluated by a neurologist** for common EDS conditions such as tethered cord, Chiari I Malformation, and instability of the neck . This is a very very important and every patient should have this evaluation and have a neurologist monitor you. Many of us need to have the tethered cord released to end issues with the bladder, kidneys, pressure in the chest, and issues with legs.

   If you test positive, get it done and then you will feel so much better and be able to progress onto physical therap more successfully. Instability of the neck will cause havoc with your body if strengthening does not succeed. Chiari I Malformation must also be addressed. Any or all of these may be an issue for you in time, but please know that correcting them when the time is right will make the difference in moving forward again.

5. **Find a good manual sacral physical therapist.** This is your chance to take better control of your life by learning, through the guidance of a manual therapist. "Living Life to the Fullest With Ehlers-Danlos Syndrome" is a new book written by my therapist, Kevin Muldowney. He learned by taking on many EDS patients at his clinic, that there are safe ways to strengthen our muscles. I have been through the protocols and have found they work for me. You'll need to stay loyal to the daily workouts. But believe me, I love being proactive and so appreciate the good that is now showing -- like having the scarum hold!

6. **Develop a network of doctors that understand EDS or are willing get educated.** Feel free to visit my website to see if a doctor is listed near you. Also feel free to contact us if you have a good doctor that we can add to the list.

   Remember, we are complicated and never get all better. That is a lot for a doctor to want to take on. Be patient and look for compatible personalities and let them learn through you.

7. **Be sure to have a cardiologist.** You should have an echocardiogram (echo test) done yearly. The test uses sound waves to produce images of the heart and allows the cardiologist to see if your heart is beating and pumping blood correctly.

8. **Determine drug and food allergies.** I wish years ago I had a clue that there was testing out there to see why I had bad reactions to some medications and foods since birth. A simple DNA drug sensitivity test can help you determine what is a safe drug to be able to put into your body. The same goes for

food sensitivity testing. You will learn what foods are causing issues or what drugs are not metabolizing. Both these issues are VERY important to address. If you keep taking medication or eating foods that are not compatible to your body, then you are adding to the inflammation in your system. More inflammation means more pain due to the increase of subluxations!

Remember, you are not alone. Find a local EDS support group and learn as much as you can as to how to live more safely with this condition.

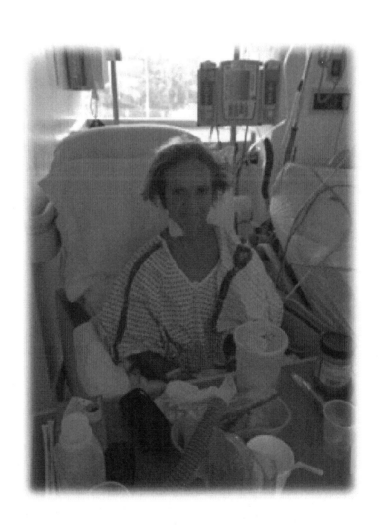

How to Stop Hospital Horrors

January 29, 2016
By Ellen Lenox Smith, Columnist

I am guessing many readers will be able to relate to this topic --
the horrors of being in a hospital with a complicated chronic
condition like mine, Ehlers-Danlos syndrome. Whether it is a
planned surgery or an emergency visit, patients who do not fit
into a "neat box" often find that staying in a hospital can be
insulting, frightening, and at times dangerous.

If you are reading this as a medical professional who works in a
hospital, I hope you will think about what it is like to be a patient
in this circumstance and consider helping to change the staff's
attitudes and ways.

I will share three short stories to help you to begin to understand
the horrors that can happen.

One of the most horrifying things my husband and I faced was
when we flew from our home state of Rhode Island to Wisconsin
to have my feet reconstructed. My life, after the surgery, was to be
five months in a wheelchair, non weight bearing. It was not an
easy assignment to face.

After the successful surgery, a hospital social worker was assigned to find a safe rehabilitation center for me until I was strong enough to travel back home.

She arrived in the room four mornings later to announce that not one place would accept me because I was "too complicated" due to my drug and food reactions. As a result, I was to be discharged to home. We were sent that afternoon to a motel that turned out to be filthy. I had to use a bedpan since I was no longer able to walk and then flew home the next day. It was humiliating and also dangerous to send me home just a few days after major surgeries, but we had nothing we could do to change this.

Lesson Learned: I did, in time, write to the president of the hospital to let him know how unacceptable this treatment was. From that point on, we were given a wonderful team to help make sure this never happened again. We have returned year after year to the same hospital for my surgeries.

Another event was dealing with IV's. Because of my condition, IV's were difficult to hold in place and many times became infiltrated, sending medication into the surrounding tissue instead of the blood stream. One night I kept telling the nurse in charge of me that the IV was dislodged. I was told all was just fine, even though as he administered the pain medication into the IV it stung and made the location of the injection swell immediately.

He said to "get some rest, you are just tired." Well, I was right, the pain medication did not get into the blood. So, I had to suffer with unnecessary pain until an ICU nurse came down and was able to successfully get the IV catheter into a vein and stay there. This all happen in the middle of the night while I was in post op, exhausted and paying the price for a nurse not willing to listen to me and take me seriously.

Lesson Learned: Today, I no longer get an IV. We either use a PIC line or port for surgeries. They hold and work for me!

My next story involves a friend who was admitted to a hospital so sick that she was not able to get out of bed without passing out and going into seizures. Due to her complications, she was not able to get the care needed and was transported to Johns Hopkins Hospital. Within 24 hours, after a standard MRI *while laying down*, it was declared that she was to sit up, take the neck collar off, and be discharged.

The problem was the only way to get a true answer for what was wrong with her was to have an MRI *while standing up*.

After much hard work by her mom and husband, my friend was transported to Doctor's Community Hospital; where it was determined, via the correct neurosurgeon who ordered the correct imaging, that she needed a neck fusion quickly to save her life. Yet, two hospitals wanted to discharge her home and felt she was just fine.

Lesson Learned: Be sure to get to a hospital that your skilled doctor has connections with. Don't give up until you find the right doctor at the right hospital, for if my friend had listened to the first two places, she would not be alive today.

So what can we all do to change the potential of inappropriate treatment, or even no treatment at all?

1. Try to deal with your difficult issues, as much as you can, at home and with doctors you can trust, instead of running to a hospital. My husband and I have a pact to stay away from hospitals as much as we can to keep me safe, even though we both admit that we would so appreciate knowing we could go there safely for help.

2. If there is no choice but to go to the hospital, come as prepared as you can with files of your medical records, including lists of medications, medications you react to, supplements, diagnosis, previous surgeries, contact info for doctors that treat you, and tests done along with their dates and locations.

3. I have a packet of all this information that we keep in the car "just in case." I also keep the records on my computer and can easily add new information when needed.

4. Make sure your doctor is part of the hospital you go to or is able to connect with the right people in the one you must get to.

5. If you have a negative experience, write the president of the hospital, not to just vent and complain, but with the intent to share issues of your care and to help educate in any way you can. Remember, if we just bad mouth them, we could potentially not be welcome at all. I had a phone call once from a local doctor who saw a negative Facebook post by a frustrated patient that included the doctor's and the hospital's names. The call was to ask me to take down the post, because the hospital staff were reading it and were really upset. The doctor told me we had to be careful how we dealt with this or people would reject taking us at all!

6. Write your congressman and share why being admitted to a hospital in their district is dangerous for you. If we don't speak out, it continues and we suffer.

Unfortunately, we walk a fine line. We need to share these horror stories, but we have to be cautious how we do this. We want changes to happen, but we don't want to turn people off by being so aggressive and so angry that they turn away from helping us or others like us in the future.

Education is constantly the theme; teach others what your condition is like, offer to speak out, and even consider a letter to the editor to share your concerns. But again, remember to think how you express these words. When somebody approaches you feeling extremely angry, you feel that vibration and want to back up. The medical team will feel this way too.

We have to be bigger people and put our anger aside to explain what it's like to be in our situation.

Success Stories of Real Medical Marijuana Patients

August 03, 2015
By Ellen Lenox Smith, Columnist

My husband and I have been licensed medical marijuana caregivers in the state of Rhode Island for over five years. Our lives have been touched by the many people who have been sent our way by doctors for education about medical marijuana. Some of the people below are either our present or past patients, along with some from other states we met and have kept in touch with.

We hope their stories will help you gain the courage to give this safe, non-invasive pain medication a try.

Bob - Paraplegic

Bob arrived at our house in his handicap equipped van and we met him in the driveway. It was difficult to understand Bob's speech at first due to his intense level of pain. He seemed overwhelmed and lost.

The doctor who saved Bob's life when he fell off a roof and was impaled and paralyzed, warned him when he awoke from surgery that he would experience intense pain for the rest of his life.

However, things changed when Bob tried medical marijuana. He vaporized marijuana right there in the driveway, proceeded to tell us that he felt no change, and before he knew it was having a conversation with us. At times, the effects of marijuana are so gentle you don't realize what is changing.

Bob became an advocate for medical marijuana and almost daily would call on the phone to make sure we were doing okay. He became a gentleman that was able to share, care and feel again.

Bob has since passed and is missed, but we know that his dignity was restored by cannabis relieving his pain. Vaporizing medical marijuana allowed Bob to have a peaceful ending.

Scott -- Multiple Sclerosis

42-year old Scott, who has a severe case of multiple sclerosis, told me that turning to medical marijuana saved his life. The former customer service representative was thrilled when he found an alternative to using Avonex for his condition. He did not like using the drug because it caused flu like symptoms and a high fever.

By smoking cannabis, Scott is able to control his pain and is thrilled how he is able to move his stiff legs. He also says it relieves his neuropathic pain too.

School Teacher – Ehlers-Danlos Syndrome

An elementary school teacher, who asked that we not use her name, was diagnosed with Ehlers-Danlos Syndrome (EDS). She was not sleeping and had a terrible time functioning in her job. Then she decided to try medical marijuana. She began taking an indica oil at night before going to bed and a sativa tincture during the day after work. Just 10 minutes after each dose, her pain levels are diminished or completely relieved.

She finds the night time dose carries into the following day, but doesn't hinder her either mentally or physically. It allows her to function and be the teacher she was before --- vibrant and focused.

"Without this gift of oils, I would be in continuous pain 24 hours a day, 365 days out of the year," she told me. "This does not change who I am. It just changes how I am, functioning and living each day, which should be to its fullest."

Lori - Spinal Injury

57-year old Lori had been employed as a medical coding technician at a local hospital. In 2007, she had an injury to her spine. Unfortunately, back surgery led to epidural fibrosis. After months of failed alternative treatments and medications, Lori's doctor suggested she try medical marijuana.

She found immense relief using a portable vaporizer (PAX) two to three times a day. Lori no longer has to rely on narcotics for pain relief and her entire lifestyle has changed.

"I have at least half of my life back," she says. "I am not severely depressed, I get out alone more often, and the pain is there but not ruling my life!"

Stryder - Ehlers-Danlos Syndrome and Epilepsy

We met 5-year old Stryder at an EDS conference in 2013. A pain clinic doctor got in touch with us after meeting with his mother, Angela.

Our hearts broke to see a gorgeous young man crippled from the joys of life by severe medical issues. Stryder barely noticed us and was not conversing. He was pale and exhausted.

We talked with Angela, gave her a donation of our night indica oil (not made from any high CBD plants) and carefully gave directions on how to use it.

They were sharing a room with a woman, and Angela told us Stryder had driven the woman crazy with the seizures he had during the night. But, after the second night of trying the oil, she asked Angela in the morning what she had done differently. When she told her the truth, the woman was amazed with the changes.

Stryder was a different boy. He was talking and interacting like he hadn't before. Angela believes this was caused by a combination of sleep and brain rest from the seizures. Stryder was alert, smiling, walking, and even went off to play with other children at the conference.

Today, Angela says Stryder is a legal marijuana patient in his state, takes his oil based medication in a dropper and sometime uses cannabis candy to suck on. He is sleeping better at night and is happier.

Angela advocates for medical marijuana to help others get educated with correct facts. When someone said they were against putting cannabis in candy, here is how she responded:

"Would you rather a child smoke it? The drugs that these kids are put on for seizures are devastating, have a lot of side effects and are addicting," Angela said. "Children are often told to just suck it up when it comes to pain management and that's just not fair. Stryder's success has been unmatched and I will always be an advocate for something that is natural and less harmful as well as effective."

Maureen – Postural Orthostatic Tachycardia Syndrome (POTS)

The day Maureen arrived to our house, we wondered how she even made it driving to us. Her POTS (a syndrome that causes an abnormally high blood pressure and heart rate) was so severe, she was shaky and extremely pale. Her cardiologist had wanted her try marijuana since he had observed other POTS patients get relief from it.

Maureen's POTS was diagnosed at age 54, where she was working as an ER technician. She chose to use the oil and the tincture as needed, until she was put into an experimental cardiac rehab program and began getting saline infusions. After several months, she found that this helped to keep her blood pressure at a normal level and made her symptoms less severe.

"When you're sick every day for a long period of time, anything that helps is worth it; not just for the physical symptoms but for your mental state as well," Maureen told me.

Today, at age 57, she no longer has to use marijuana at all. She keeps her symptoms under control with exercise and saline infusions. However, if the need arrives again, Maureen says she wouldn't hesitate to use marijuana again.

Bonnie - Pudendal Neuralgia and Post-Fusion Pain

At 75, retired college professor Bonnie arrived at our home in severe pain. After much education and consideration, she decided to give medical marijuana a try.

In time, as she gained her confidence, Bonnie found that eating brownies with marijuana, along with taking indica oil at night, provided her relief from unrelenting pain. It also provided some hope, thus improving her outlook on life.

"The only real relief I have had from my pain has been with medical marijuana. My medicine allows me to enjoy life again," Bonnie says.

Elizabeth - Chronic Regional Pain Syndrome, EDS and Chiari Malformation

29-year old Elizabeth was sent to us by a pain clinic doctor. This beautiful, terribly thin, and discouraged young lady and her mother arrived at our home and it broke our heart. Elizabeth's CRSP was so severe on her head that she was no longer able to touch it, let alone consider running a comb or brush through her hair.

Elizabeth was a former piano teacher and a recording artist, struggling to hold onto her career. She clearly wanted to get back control of her life. While in our home, she started to rub our topical on her scalp and we were startled when she said she felt some immediate relief. So began her magical way to help get some quality of her life back.

Elizabeth now administers her medical marijuana in a variety of ways. She eats it with edibles, drinks it, massages her joints with it, vaporizes it, and occasionally smokes it. She enjoys using a Magical Butter machine that it makes potent tinctures and oils, and appreciates the "no heat" option, which she uses to make CannaMilk.

Elizabeth found she requires high doses of THC, because she doesn't absorb it at a normal rate. As a slow absorber, she doesn't get a big peak in relief, followed by a sharp drop-off. Instead it gives her a pretty consistent relief and doesn't make her feel "stoned."

With medical marijuana, she feels her muscles are not as rigid. She can relax, sleep better, and can touch areas of her skin that used to be too sensitive to touch.

"It has changed my life for the better," Elizabeth says.

Melvin - Renal Failure, Degenerative Lumbar Disc, PTSD, Headaches

43-year old Melvin is employed as an agricultural-inspector. We met this very intelligent, kind man at our home a few years ago and hoped that using medical marijuana would provide the relief he needed to be able to function better in life.

Melvin did a lot of research about how to use marijuana, what strains to consider, and in time found the best way for him to administer it was with vaporizing and using extracts.

He found that his PTSD was mostly relieved by using the higher CBD strains. Melvin's PTSD causes unwanted and uncontrollable visions and thoughts. Marijuana slows them down, without triggering emotional responses. It's not a cure for his PTSD, but has made it more manageable.

There are two damaged discs causing nerve pain which radiate down Melvin's legs – making them feel numb, burning and painful. He alleviates this pain using marijuana strains like Bubble Gum, Lucy and Pineapple Express. Without them, Melvin says his back would be in constant pain and he would have to lie in bed for most of the day. With marijuana, he is a functioning employed worker.

"With a huge help from my caregiver I was able to find the correct THC to CBD ratio that works for my PTSD and disc/nerve degeneration. Medical marijuana is my freedom!" Melvin says.

Bill - Cardiac Issues

We met Bill and his wife, Joan, a few years ago. Despite his failing health, the love and commitment between them was so clear. We hoped that medical marijuana would provide the relief needed to allow Bill dignity with the time left in his life.

A former firefighter for 30 years, Bill was diagnosed with just 20% cardiac output. This caused him severe pain while breathing.

Bill found that administering the marijuana in an oil night and using the tincture during the day gave him relief. He was able to sleep again for more than one or two hours. For the severe pain in the center of his ribcage, due to an unhealed fracture, the topical cream gave Bill relief that lasted for hours.

Bill used this form of medication for about a year and wished he had been able to use it even sooner, so that he could have had a better quality of life.

Sadly, Bill recently passed away at the age of 73.

Diana - Ehlers-Danlos Syndrome

53-year old Diana was a national award-winning composer, pianist, singer, violinist, dancer, and actress. She had to turn down a Master's fellowship because of her recurrent back, shoulder, and elbow/wrist pain. Instead, she worked as lab technician.

Cortisone shots and bed rest were the "treatment" for her pain. For five long years, she wore hard braces from her wrists to her elbows, yet also managed to perform lead roles in musicals (with braces hidden beneath costumes).

After she was finally diagnosed with EDS, she turned to medical marijuana two years ago. Now, every night, Diana uses an indica oil. Without it, she would sweat throughout the night profusely. Medical marijuana has also reduced her pain from EDS.

Sally - Stage IV Cancer

Courageous 71-year old Sally has been successfully using medical marijuana for over five years. She began using it after being diagnosed with Stage IV uterine cancer.

Sally has defied all odds by remaining active and engaged in life. She found that using the oil at night gave her much needed quality sleep and lowered her pain. For daytime relief, she found vaporizing controlled her nausea.

"Marijuana has few, if no side effects. It is benign in terms of overall functioning," she says.

We lost Sally, this past year, but she will always be a role model to us all; determined, positive and caring. She touched lives in a positive way and will always be in the hearts of those that have had the honor to know her.

These are just a few of the amazing success stories that I have experienced with patients using medical marijuana. Most people that try marijuana are able to find relief from the different conditions they are striving to live a better life with.

We look forward to the future when more research is allowed in our country. This, in turn, would provide the needed support and education for those in the medical field, so they could understand

and encourage their patients to try marijuana. Not as a last resort, but as the first choice.

Staying Positive But Still Needing Support

February 17, 2016
By Ellen Lenox Smith, Columnist

It took over 50 years for me to be diagnosed correctly and to finally understand what I have been suffering from for so many years – sarcoidosis and Ehlers-Danlos syndrome. The latter is actually something that I was born with.

Every day of my life, I have to work to get through the day in as positive way as I can muster. Yet, it is clear people still don't understand how brave I am trying to be. I am still in need of support. I live with two incurable, painful conditions that will keep progressing.

Despite these diagnoses, last month I was discharged by a nurse from a support organization called Vital Decisions. After taking me on as a client on their own initiative last April, it was stated that their requirements had changed to continue with a client.

Since they believe I am doing a good job, with my husband managing my health and making the necessary decisions one has to face, I no longer qualify for their support.

Believe me, I knew where this conversation was going, for this was not the first time this has happened to me. You put on a smile, adopt a positive attitude, take on your health conditions, work hard to live life with them; and then someone assumes you must be all set and you are sent off on your own. Something is just wrong with this process.

With long term chronic pain, others need to understand that even those of us presenting positively still need their support. It takes a lot of work to keep the spirits up, act pleasant around you, and act like life is normal. Don't think we aren't at times scared, overtired, and overwhelmed from living with pain.

And believe me, even on our good days, you would not want to climb into our bodies. So, we still need you to care about us!

I have had friends disappear since my story is too sad to be around. I have also had to live with judgement due to my smile -- which is seen as a sign that I must be doing just fine. But would you rather have me be that miserable person that is angry, lashing out at others, and giving up on finding purpose and meaning to my life?

And, how is it that in that same week I got discharged from Vital Decisions, another doctor sent me a note that his practice is putting me in their new program called the Specialty Care Center, which will help support me with my cardiac issues? Am I the same person that just got let go by my support nurse?

If you see someone you know coping with a difficult medical issue, please don't assume that they are just fine if they have a smile on their face. Ask them how they are doing, let them vent, care about them, and be proud of them for trying to get through a difficult journey while being pleasant.

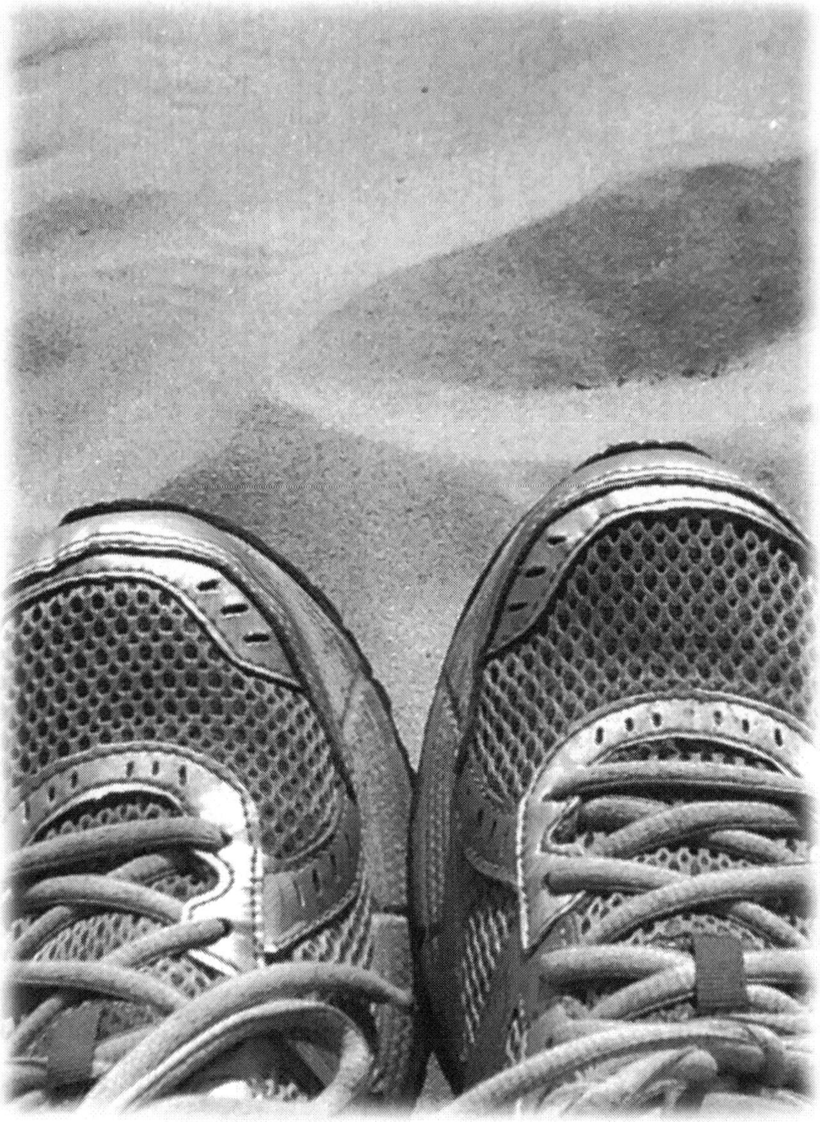

Why You Should Consider Medical Marijuana

May 01, 2015

(Editor's note: Pain News Network is pleased to welcome Ellen Lenox Smith as our newest columnist. Ellen has suffered from chronic pain all of her life, but it wasn't until a few years ago that she discovered the pain relieving benefits of medical marijuana. In future columns, Ellen will focus on marijuana and how it can be used as pain medication. Medical marijuana is legal in 23 U.S. states and the District of Columbia. But even in states where it is legal, doctors may frown upon marijuana and drop patients from their practice for using it.)

By Ellen Lenox Smith, Columnist

Why -- at the age of 57 -- would one ever consider turning to medical marijuana?

I wondered the same thing after being sent to a pain doctor just before another surgery in 2006. After reviewing my records and seeing that I was unresponsive to pain medication, the doctor clearly had no idea what to suggest, except trying medical marijuana.

I was born with Ehlers-Danlos syndrome and later also added sarcoidosis to my life. I was living with chronic pain that was preventing me from sleeping, thinking straight, and functioning.

From birth, I had one issue after another reacting to medications. And after 22 surgeries, you can imagine the horror of all I had to endure and the added pain of never knowing the proper relief my body could have from pain medication. Eventually, a DNA drug sensitivity test was ordered and it confirmed I could not metabolize most drugs. This meant no aspirin, Tylenol, or any opiates.

I took the advice to try medical marijuana with tremendous trepidation. At that time in Rhode Island, you either had to grow your own or buy it on the black market. Since growing takes about three months, I decided the only way to find out what marijuana would do for me was to find a source and give it a try.

When I was able to find some marijuana, I ground it up, heated up some olive oil and let it release the medicine into the oil. I had no choice, since I was told by a pulmonologist that smoking marijuana with sarcoidosis in the chest would be fatal. I wanted to try a different way to administer it.

That night, I measured out one teaspoon of the infused oil. I mixed it with some applesauce and one hour before bedtime, I swallowed it down. I remember being scared -- for I am not one that likes to be out of control of my body. Having smoked marijuana once in college, I hated that sensation.

As soon as I took the dose, I went to my husband and warned him that I had taken marijuana and to keep an eye out for me. I was convinced this was a stupid thing to be doing and I would be stoned all night.

One hour later, we got in bed, I closed my eyes and before I knew it, it was morning. I had slept the whole night, never waking up once!

I woke up refreshed, not groggy, and ready to take on life again. I had no "high" or stoned sensation like you would guess would happen.

I learned quickly that someone in pain does not react the same way to cannabis as someone who uses it for recreational reasons. The brain receptors connect with the THC and cannabinoids (the active ingredients in marijuana), and provide safe and gentle pain relief.

I was shocked and thrilled with the result. My husband and I quickly got to work setting up a legal way to grow marijuana. I realized that life was directing us to new topic we just had to advocate for.

If I was scared to try marijuana, there is no question that others felt the same way -- and we had to let them know how amazing it really is. Society brought us up to be negative about marijuana, yet it was used in our country many years ago and even sold in pharmacies. The success of this medication was squashed, and we were all led to believe that it was bad and dangerous.

What we learned is that no one dies from using marijuana, no one develops organ damage, and with a body in chronic pain -- you can regain your life back.

Are my conditions cured? No, they are both incurable. But I have been able to advocate, think, feel and live again thanks to using medical marijuana.

Don't be scared. Consider how much safer this medication is than all the other pain relief choices out there. Turn your body and your life with pain around. You won't regret it.

How to Use Medical Marijuana without Smoking

June 03, 2015
By Ellen Lenox Smith, Columnist

It can be overwhelming to try anything new, especially something like medical marijuana. Many people are afraid to try it – not only because of the stigma associated with cannabis – but the smell that comes from smoking it.

There are many different ways besides smoking that I have learned to administer medical marijuana. But remember, I am not an expert, just a woman who was desperately trying to find a solution as to how to address her pain. I have been learning this slowly, through reading, help from others, and trial and error.

Due to having sarcoidosis in my chest, smoking anything could be fatal. I had to find an alternative method that I could use to safely administer medical marijuana. Acting on the advice of a friend, I started my journey utilizing this medicine in an oil form.

Oils

I start by grinding up dried marijuana buds in a simple coffee grinder, always being careful to use only an indica strain of cannabis. Indica plants give you pain relief and allow you to rest. I take my oil at night to help me to sleep. If I ever took this same oil during the day, I would be sleepy and groggy.

Next, I heat up oil (I use extra virgin olive oil, but you can use other types you prefer) and when it gets hot, but not to a boil, I sprinkle the ground product over the oil. When you get it just right, there is a sound similar to putting an Alka Seltzer tablet in water, and you can hear the THC and CBD being released into the oil.

You then allow the oil to cool, strain it, and store it away from the sun. It lasts for a long time.

At night, one hour before I want to go to sleep, I take my medication. I presently use one teaspoon of the oil mixed with some applesauce or something I enjoy eating. You do not want to take this on an empty stomach.

You should start slowly with a small amount, and gradually introduce the medication to your body. If you need to increase the dose, you can add a quarter of a teaspoon until you have reached an appropriate level. When you can sleep through the night, and awake relatively clear headed and not groggy --then you know your dose is appropriate.

Keep in mind that by utilizing this method the medication takes time to kick in because it is being ingested. Plan your evening carefully and be sure to be ready for bed once you have medicated. It usually takes 30-60 minutes. We all react differently, so be safe.

If you want to make this oil even easier, then purchase a machine called Magical Butter, and it will do all the work for you after you grind, measure and plug it in. It costs about $175.

Vaporizers

Most days, I do not need any medication after having had a good night's sleep. But on the days I need something else for help, I find vaporizing simple and easy.

I have found two portable vaporizers that I love. One is called the Vape-or-Smoke and the other is named PAX. They require a small amount of marijuana, are small enough to fit in a purse, and are simple to use.

Many people use the Volcano, which is a larger, table top model seen in the picture to the right. There are so many types; you just have to decide what you are willing to spend. Some vaporizers cost several hundred dollars.

Now be careful, for you want to vaporize the correct type of cannabis. I could list all fifteen strains we grow, but I can tell you that there would be no guarantee they would be your magic.

The main thing to remember is if you are going to vaporize during the day, then you need to use a sativa strain of cannabis. This type of plant allows you to gain pain relief and also helps to stimulate you and keep you awake, not sleep like the indica plant does. If I vaporized an indica during the day, I would want to sleep. So be careful you have selected the correct type of plant.

Use a grinder to prepare the marijuana and follow the directions on the vaporizer. You will notice when you first use a vaporizer that it looks like you are blowing out smoke. However, what you are observing is actually a vapor.

I have permission from my pulmonologist to vaporize because it is safe to use. Take a simple hit, see how you feel in a few minutes, and if you need more to help with the pain, just use it one puff at a time to find your needed dose. This method should provide you with short, yet quick relief, unlike the oil that takes awhile to kick in, but last so much longer.

Tinctures

Sometimes I also use a tincture during the day. As with vaporizing, it is fast acting and also fast to leave the system. We have recipes for a few types. One is made with alcohol, such as lemon schnapps and it takes two months to cure. The other is made with glycerin and can be made in less than an hour in a crock pot or using the Magical Butter machine.

When making a tincture, you again have to be careful you are using the correct strain. I make day tincture, so I only use a sativa plant. Alcohol based tinctures require the product to be put into a jar, the alcohol of choice poured over it, and then covered tightly.

Twice a day, take a moment to shake the jar. After two months, the THC and CBD are released, and you should strain and store the liquid away from the sun.

The tincture can be taken one teaspoon at a time or with an eyedropper, putting a few drops under the tongue or in the side of the cheek. You hold it there for about 20 seconds and then swallow. Feel free to repeat this every half hour. Remember, this is made with the plant that stimulates, so do not take at night!

The glycerin recipe is easy and can be made in an hour using a crock pot. You administer it the same way as above. The difference with this method is it has no alcohol and tastes sweet -- even though a diabetic can use it for it is not sugar based.

It's just a matter of preference of which type you prefer and how long you want to wait for the finished product to use.

Topical Ointments

We have had good success using topical ointments. The recipes are simple and the results are amazing. I know people with Complex Regional Pain Syndrome who have turned their lives around with topicals.

All it requires is the tincture (not the oil), some bees wax, and then we add essential oils to mask any marijuana odor. Peppermint extract seems to be the favorite additive -- it provides a tingling sensation as it absorbs into the skin along with the cannabis.

Recipes for topicals, tinctures, and oils can all be found on our website at the end of this article.

As stated in the beginning, I am not an expert on all the various way to administer medical marijuana. Many people love using edibles, such as brownies and cookies, but I live with so many food allergies that I have no interest in even trying them.

It also concerns me, being so drug reactive, how much I should eat or not eat because I don't feel the effects immediately. Like the oil, edibles are slow to activate and sometimes people eat more than they should -- and suddenly they're shocked at how strange they feel.

Go slowly and give it time to kick in before deciding you need to eat more!

We try to steer people away from smoking to keep the lungs as safe as possible. However, if that is the only way that works for you and the smell is not an issue for you, then smoking is one of the faster ways to get pain relief from marijuana.

Other Suggestions
To Consider:

Vecttor Treatments

Dr Donald A. Rhodes;
drrhodes2@aol.com
http://www.alanneuromedical.com/contact/

NEADS – Service, Therapy And Hearing Dogs

P.O. Box 213
West Boylston, Massachusetts 01583
978-422-9064
jmoon@neads.org

Good Dog Blanket - To Protect Your Car

http://www.gooddogblanket.com
name Annemarie Feeley
phone: 508-245-1532

Who Can You Turn To For Help?
Doctors who specialize in helping Ehlers-Danlos patients

Check the list that is constantly being updated of doctors that are trying to help those with EDS found on our web site: https://ellenandstuartsmith.squarespace.com/eds/

Just click on the following and it will open at the bottom of your computer.

DNA Drug Sensitivity Testing

What you need to know about personalized prescribing

800-TEST-DNA ; 800-837-8362 or visit online at www.HealthandDNA.com

for more information.

GeneMedsRX can help you minimize the risk of adverse drug reactions

(ADRS). ADRS are the fourth to sixth greatest killer in the U.S. with more than 100,000 deaths per year. These are not errors; they occur within the FDA-approved dosage and labeling recommendations. Many may be preventable if potential drug-drug and drug-gene interaction risks

TROUBLE SLEEPING?

Contact your primary care doctor for a script for an air mattress to help with controlling subluxations at night.

CONSIDER SLEEPING GROUNDED

http://www.earthing.com/Default.asp

Throughout history humans walked barefoot and slept on the ground. But modern lifestyle, including the widespread use of insulative rubber- or plastic-soled shoes, has disconnected us from the Earth's energy and, of course, we no longer sleep on the ground. Fascinating new research has raised the possibility that this disconnect may actually contribute to chronic pain, fatigue, and poor sleep that plague so many people.

The remedy for the disconnect is simple. Walk barefoot outdoors whenever possible and/or sleep, work, or relax indoors in contact with conductive sheets or mats that transfer the energy to your body. People who do on a regular basis say they sleep better, feel better, and have more energy during the day. This simple practice is called Earthing, also known as grounding, and it is both a technology and a movement which is transforming lives across the planet.

Earthing is safe and natural, for people of all ages, young and old, but it is not medicine or a

substitute for medical treatment. If you have a medical condition, see your physician or healthcare provider.

HOW TO EXPERIENCE EARTHING...NOW

Go barefoot outside for a half-hour and see what a difference it makes on your pain or stress level. Sit, stand, or walk on grass, sand, dirt, or concrete. These are all conductive surfaces from which your body can draw the Earth's energy. Wood, asphalt, and vinyl won't work. They are not conductive surfaces. Experience for yourself the healing energy of the Earth at work.

Camp for Kids!

The Coalition Against Pediatric Pain (TCAPP), RSDSA, and the US Pain Foundation partnered with The Center for Courageous

Kids in Kentucky to create a camp for kids in pain.

The Center for Courageous Kids is located in Scottsville, Kentucky.

To learn more about the camp location and what they have to offer, please visit The Center for Courageous Kids website at: http://www.thecenterforcourageouskids.org.

Contact The Author:

Ellen Lenox Smith suffers from Ehlers-Danlos Syndrome and sarcoidosis.

ELLEN LENOX SMITH

Ellen and her husband Stuart live in Rhode Island. They are co-directors for medical marijuana advocacy for the U.S. Pain Foundation and serve as board members for the Rhode Island Patient Advocacy Coalition.

**For more information about medical marijuana,
and to contact the author, visit her website:**

http://ellenandstuartsmith.squarespace.com/

I am standing,
watching from a distance
as my husband and my service dog enjoy the wet sand and the surf.
The sneakers on the sand are mine.
I am dreaming.
I wish could walk again on sand.

I will never again be able to walk barefoot in the sand without shoes.
or anywhere without shoes.
Sand and beach was a big part of my life...

One of the many things I have had to give up.

I challenge you!

Next time you are sick or injured...

- Discover how you can help find purpose and meaning back in your life.
- Learn how it is possible to accept your pain but not give in to it.

Made in the USA
San Bernardino, CA
28 August 2017